ON SOLID GROUND

Tom Osborne

Edited and with photographs by Gordon Thiessen

UNIVERSITY OF NEBRASKA PRESS
LINCOLN AND LONDON

Library of Congress Cataloging-in-Publication Data
Osborne, Tom, 1937–
On solid ground / Tom Osborne; edited and with photographs by
Gordon Thiessen.
p. cm.
Originally published: Lincoln: Nebraska Book Pub., c1996.
ISBN 978-0-8032-7147-0 (pbk.: alk. paper)
1. Osborne, Tom, 1937– 2. Nebraska Cornhuskers (Football team)
3. University of Nebraska (Lincoln campus)—Football. I. Thiessen, Gordon.
II. Title.
GV958.U53O73   2012
796.332'6309782293—dc23
2012017205

Dedication

This book is dedicated to the players and coaches of the 1993, 1994 and 1995 teams. These teams have shown outstanding focus, commitment and dedication to excellence.

CONTENTS

ACKNOWLEDGMENTS

I would like to acknowledge my secretary, Mary Lyn Wininger, for doing much of the typing and also for helping to edit the manuscript, Gordon Thiessen for his work in providing photographs and editing, to the Nebraska Bookstore and Martha Hoppe for the efforts that they have provided in proofreading, producing and publishing the book and to my wife, Nancy, for her timely suggestions and her consistent support.

FOREWORD

On April 26, 1996, a talk show on Boston station WEEI asked me to be on their program. They wanted to talk about a former player, Christian Peter. Normally, I don't appear on talk shows, but I thought this might give me a chance to clarify Christian's off-the-field problems. He had just been drafted by the New England Patriots and was then abruptly dropped by them because of his "past." Therefore, in an attempt to help Christian, I agreed to go on the show. I told the contact person that I would be on the air for just a few minutes, would not take phone calls from listeners and would give them a statement concerning Christian.

About an hour later, the radio station's contact person called back. As I waited on the line for my turn on the program, I heard one of the announcers state something to the effect that they would soon be hearing from a coach who allows players who beat up women to play on his team. Needless to say, I knew this interview might get rough. When I went on the air with the two announcers, Eddie Andelman and Dale Arnold, I made the comment that I had agreed to come on the air only to talk about Christian Peter. Then I gave them a brief sketch of what Christian was like from my point of view. Suddenly, Andelman flew off the handle. He said I was a disgrace to college football, I was a "b— s—er," and that he was going to leave the room. As he turned the interview over to the other announcer, I could hear him yelling as he walked out. I was amazed at this whole turn of events. The whole episode was so bizarre I almost started laughing. The interview was revealing in several respects. First, it showed how thin the veil of common courtesy has become. Second, it illustrated how eager some are to develop opinions based on very few facts. Third, it showed how badly the image of our football team, and my image as well, had been tarnished during the 1995 football season.

Because of our back-to-back national championship titles, we've had more fans and media take notice of our football program. This added scrutiny, at times, has been flattering and, at times, has been annoying. I doubt that Eddie Andelman knows very much about Nebraska football other than what has recently appeared in some national media coverage. Based on his reaction to me and the football program there isn't much doubt that he has formed a very negative opinion of us. I doubt this book will do much to change the thinking of the Eddie Andelmans of the world. For those people who have labeled us as a win-at-all-cost football program, little can be done to change their minds. However, there are many people who really don't know much about Nebraska football or what has gone on in this program behind the scenes in recent years and who have open minds. It is for these people that this book was written. I am confident that it provides an accurate portrayal of what has happened to our team during the past few years.

I would not feel right about benefiting financially from this undertaking as the true authors of this book are the players, coaches and support staff who have worked so hard to enable our program to be successful. Most of my proceeds from the sale of this book will go to charitable causes.

I hope telling our story will help people become more familiar with the philosophical principles that have guided our program consistently over a period of years. There are many who disagree with these principles. However, I think that it is important that they be carefully examined before being dismissed as "self-serving" and "win-at-all-costs."

This book also attempts to delve into some issues facing our nation, and particularly our young people, as they attempt to move through a very difficult time in the history of our country. I believe that the players who participate in the Nebraska program reflect our society. Many of them have overcome great odds to have achieved what they have accomplished, both on and off the field.

We have received a great deal of criticism for the misbehavior of a few. There is a good deal of controversy over how those who misbehave on an athletic team should be treated. On the one hand, there are those who feel that an athlete who is in trouble should be made an example and should be cut off from any affiliation with the athletic team thereby "sending a message" deterring others from following in the offender's footsteps. On the other hand, there is the viewpoint that part of being human is to make mistakes. Giving those who have made a poor decision a chance to rectify their mistakes in a structured environment is the best way to ensure growth and a lasting change in behavior. One fundamental question considered in this book is how to resolve the tension between the two points of view.

Football teams are composed of human beings. It is a common practice to dehumanize athletes and see them only as objects whose sole purpose is to entertain. Hopefully, this book will help dispel this myth, as athletes have the same emotions and problems that others have.

I have great admiration for the typical major college football player today. He is under much scrutiny and has many academic, athletic and social demands placed upon him. In some ways he is asked to be all things to all people. To survive these expectations takes an exceptional human being. I trust the readers will sense that with winning comes a great deal of joy and exhilaration—and also a great deal of scrutiny that is often difficult to bear.

1

COMING CLOSER

*I*t was the best of times, it was the worst of times . . .
Charles Dickens opened his novel *A Tale of Two Cities* with
those words. They also describe my feelings about the past few
seasons at the University of Nebraska.

These have been the best of times. We have won 25 straight
football games, 36 of the last 37 games played, five straight Big
Eight Championships and two consecutive national championships. On the other hand, these have been the worst of times. Our
program has been bashed by the national media. We went from
being perceived as a highly respected football program to a win-
at-all-costs, out-of-control, football program like several other
troubled college teams. It's not been easy to be the target of so
much criticism. We have always taken pride in running a program
where the players do well academically, keep the rules, conduct
themselves properly on the field and win football games.

In athletics, when you're successful, you're subject to a lot of media attention. Initially, there is a honeymoon period during which the media builds you up. This is exactly what happened in the months following our national championship in 1994. It was the first national championship for us in 23 years and it followed our near-upset of Florida State in the Orange Bowl. I often remarked to my wife, Nancy, that things were going too smoothly, that we could do no wrong, that it couldn't last—and it didn't.

A few years ago, Mike Ditka, former coach of the Chicago Bears, reminded me that the press will build you up only to later cut you down. I have thought a lot about his comment in recent months.

In his book *Sacred Hoops,* Phil Jackson, the Chicago Bulls' head coach, relates a quote from Michael Jordan dealing with the same subject. "The media helps you become famous, but after you reach a certain level, they break you down bit by bit. It's a contradiction." Criticism doesn't occur in a vacuum; there is generally some reason for the criticism. Yet it often takes on a life of its own and can become excessive. There is a tendency to be given either a white hat or a black hat with no middle ground. I recently met a Penn State fan in the Philadelphia airport. When he discovered who I was, he suggested the media often likes to "paint the white hat black." I knew exactly what he meant.

The successes of the past three seasons haven't occurred entirely by chance. As it often happens, adversity was the springboard that contributed to our success. We lost bowl games following the 1987, 1988, 1989, 1990, 1991, 1992 and 1993 seasons. This had to be some kind of record. We were Big Eight Champions in 1988, 1991, 1992 and 1993. Our team never won fewer than nine games in any of those seasons in which we lost bowl games. We even won 11 games in 1988 and 1993. Two of the bowl losses were to Miami in 1989 and 1992 when we played on Miami's home field. When we played Georgia Tech in 1991, they were undefeated and playing for the national championship. We played well enough to beat Florida State in the 1988 Fiesta Bowl, but unfortunately we lost a close game 31-28. The paper tiger image grew because we couldn't win the "big one." I was even labeled as being a coach who couldn't win key games in a *Sports Illustrated* article. The author was a writer who primarily wrote about horse races but suddenly had become an expert on college football. Though we won enough games to stay employed, it was difficult to live with all of the criticism about not winning the "big one." But we kept plugging away and continued to learn from our losses.

While playing Florida teams, we realized speed was essential, and intensified our efforts to recruit players who could run. Following one bowl loss, a writer from Florida asked why we and other schools from the north couldn't see the light and recruit faster players like the Florida schools. I was both amused and irritated by his question. Every college football coach knows he needs the fastest players available. However, there are only a few players who have the kind of speed and talent that makes them stand out from the rest. Of course, nearly everyone is after those players. In recent years, either through diligence or good fortune, we have successfully recruited more players who can run well, particularly on defense. A good example was the 1995 Big Eight Defensive Newcomer of the Year, Terrell Farley. He was an undersized junior college linebacker who was recruited primarily by the University of Cincinnati and Nebraska. We felt his speed and movement were what we needed at linebacker. Many schools steered clear of Terrell because of his size. Most coaches thought 200 pounds was too light to play linebacker, but he came to Nebraska and made an immediate impact in our program.

We also were becoming a better team due to a change in defensive philosophy following the 1992 season. We had always operated primarily out of a 5-man defensive front with a nose tackle lined up on the center, defensive tackles lined up on the offensive tackles and defensive ends outside the tackles. Our two linebackers were lined up over the offensive guards. This type of front was effective but presented problems when we played teams that passed a great deal. We were seeing more of these teams each year—particularly in the bowl games. It became more difficult to find defensive ends who could do all of the things we required at that position in the 5-2 defense. Sometimes we were asking the defensive ends to rush the passer. Other times they were responsible for dropping into zone pass coverage. Occasionally, they even had to play a receiver in man-to-man pass coverage. It was difficult to find an athlete who could handle all the physical and mental demands of this complex position.

In the late 1980s we began to play a "dime," or 4-3 defense. In this defense we take out a defensive lineman and a linebacker and put two extra defensive backs in the game. We attempted to prepare our defense to play both the 5-2 and the 4-3 defense. Since we couldn't predict whether the offense would pass or run, we needed to have both ready. We found it was difficult to properly prepare our defense because our practice time was split between the 5-2 and the 4-3 defenses. Trying to blend the two defenses resulted in some uncertainty and confusion.

The turning point for our program came in the 1992 game against the University of Oklahoma in Norman. During the first half, Oklahoma moved the ball almost at will against our basic 5-2 defense by simply running the ball right at it. The 5-2 was designed to stop the run, so we were scrambling for a way to slow down Oklahoma. Fortunately, in the first half they made mistakes and so hadn't scored many points, but because of the way they were moving the ball and controlling the game, things looked bleak. Late in the first half we went with our dime defense, mainly because we didn't know what else to try. It was a desperate move but for some reason it confused them. We began to stop them and went on to win easily in the second half. So we decided to risk scrapping our standard 5-2 defense and adopted the 4-3 as our base defense. We hoped we could still stop the run and have a better chance to defend the pass. We hated to move away from a defensive scheme that had been so good to us over the years, but we were also convinced it was time to make the switch. By using the 4-3 defense exclusively, we hoped to make our defense simpler and our practices less confusing.

As we moved to the 4-3 for the 1993 season, we were committed to placing more emphasis on speed. A real plus was the luxury of being able to have Trev Alberts, an All-American defensive end and subsequent first-round draft choice in the NFL, available to rush the passer all of the time. Trev had dropped into pass coverage about half the time in the 5-2 scheme. Trev's greatest strength was his ability to rush the passer, so it came as no surprise when he became such a dominant player in the 4-3 defense. He recorded 15 sacks and 96 tackles during the 1993 season. In our 14-13 win over UCLA in 1993, he played perhaps the greatest game a defensive player ever played at Nebraska. Trev made plays all over the field and established himself as one of the best players in college football. He went on to win the Butkus Award, which is given each year to the outstanding college linebacker or defensive end.

Our defense went from good to great in the Orange Bowl game following the 1993 season. We shut down the Florida State offense which was led by their Heisman Trophy winner Charlie Ward. The Florida State offense had averaged over 548 yards per game and 43.3 points per game. Yet we neutralized their powerful offense and held them to 18 points.

Some controversy arose before we played Florida State in the Orange Bowl. We were 11-0 and ranked No. 1, and West Virginia, also 11-0, was ranked No. 2 or No. 3 depending on which poll you consulted. Florida State was 11-1, having lost to Notre Dame late in the season. Normally, a team that loses a game late in the season, drops enough in the polls to be removed from contention for the national championship. However, there was pressure from some in the national media to have Florida State in the national championship game. Many journalists believed Florida State was the best team in the country, despite their late season loss. The final poll, before the bowl games, showed Nebraska as No. 1, Florida State No. 2 and West Virginia No. 3.

Frankly, I wanted to play West Virginia. We wanted to play another team from a northern climate that played its home games on artificial turf. Instead, we would play another Florida team that played on grass in front of a largely Florida State crowd in the Orange Bowl. I felt badly for Don Nehlen, the West Virginia coach, because it was nearly unprecedented for a team with a loss late in the season to be ranked ahead of an unbeaten team.

Though ranked ahead of Florida State, we were 17-point underdogs. We were held up to national ridicule as no match for the Seminoles. One writer argued that we had no more than two or three players who could play for Florida State on our whole team. Most people thought this would be just another bowl game where a Florida team would run circles around a slower Husker team.

While preparing for the Orange Bowl, something happened during practice that affected the entire team. Three days before the game we were in sweat clothes and had a light practice as we were tapering off for the game. Lance Lundberg, a captain and starting offensive tackle, hit one of our scout team players, Leslie Dennis, with a blind-side block that both shocked and flattened him. Leslie was angry and looked for Lance after the practice was over. Leslie blind-sided Lance in the locker room with a punch in the eye. The episode caused some division within the team. Some players backed Lance, some backed Leslie and a great many were neutral. I sent Leslie home from the bowl site and then asked Lance to talk to the entire team. After the next practice, he apologized for his part in the altercation and urged the team to pull together. After that, the team resumed its focus on the game.

The game that followed was one of the proudest, and yet saddest, of my coaching career. Our team gave a great effort and did most of the things you have to do to win. Our offense totaled more yards than Florida State, 389 to 333. We pressured Charlie Ward the entire game. And we didn't allow him to scramble for big gains as he had against other teams. Our kicking game was also solid. We even had a 71-yard punt return by Corey Dixon in the first quarter for an apparent touchdown. It was called back on a clipping penalty that we were not able to detect on film. Still, we took the lead 16-15 with 1:16 remaining in the game on Byron Bennett's 27-yard field goal. It looked like we were finally going to win our first national championship in 22 years.

Unfortunately, the following kickoff went out of bounds giving Florida State good field position at their 35-yard line. They were forced to go for a first down on fourth and one at mid-field and they barely made it. They benefited from a 15-yard penalty when one of our defensive backs hit a Florida State receiver out of bounds. Eventually they kicked a 22-yard field goal with 21 seconds left to take the lead 18-16.

But we weren't done yet. Tommie Frazier hit Trumane Bell with a 29-yard pass giving us a chance to win on a 45-yard field goal with one second remaining. The field goal was wide to the left. Our holder on the field goal was flattened by one of their rush people, but there was no call, and the game ended with Bobby Bowden winning his first national championship. As I walked off the field, I felt badly for our team. They had played with such tenacity and commitment that it was a shame we couldn't have won the game. We had played the best team in college football and had come very close to upsetting them.

I was happy for Bobby Bowden. He had heard the same question I had over and over. As he mentions in his book *More Than Just A Game*, "Folks would ask, 'Bobby, aren't you just devastated because you've never won a national championship?' I would say, 'Naw I'm not devastated. I am disappointed because I'm a competitor. Sure I want one. I want one bad, but I ain't gonna cut my wrists because we've never won a national championship. I'd much rather have a program that goes 11-1, 10-2, 10-2, and maybe 9-3 every year than I would have one that goes 12-0 and wins it all one year, and then goes 5-6, 6-5, and 7-4 after that. I'd much rather be consistent because when you're consistent, you win a lot more than you lose.' "

From that night on January 1, 1994, through the beginning of the 1994 season, there was a great commitment to complete our unfinished business—a national championship. There was also a great feeling of confidence that it would happen. The decision to change our defense, the success in recruiting many talented players with speed, and the 1994 Orange Bowl game provided the key elements for the back-to-back national championship seasons in 1994 and 1995. We would not lose again during the careers of sophomores Tommie Frazier, Brook Berringer, Aaron Graham, Tyrone Williams, Christian Peter, Phil Ellis, Doug Colman, Tony Veland, Mark Gilman, Steve Ott, Reggie Baul, Clester Johnson and Jeff Makovicka.

2

THE
PERFECT SEASON

Before the start of the 1994 season, Bill Byrne, our athletic director, approached me about playing in the Kickoff Classic football game in late August in East Rutherford, New Jersey. We had played in the Kickoff Classic twice before and were eligible to play once every six years. Since this was our sixth year, we had to decide whether we wanted to play again. Our coaches and I agreed to play in the game if we would play West Virginia. I was confident that we would have no problem playing well against a good team early in the season. With an experienced quarterback returning and several other key players also returning, I knew we were ready to play. Nebraska and West Virginia were both undefeated and probably should have played for the national championship the previous year.

The game appealed to both West Virginia and the Kickoff Classic officials. We were scheduled to play on August 28. We had previously beaten Penn State in the 1983 Kickoff Classic 44-6.

That was the year after Penn State had won the national championship. We beat Texas A & M in the 1988 Kickoff Classic 23-14.

The Kickoff Classic was played on a hot and humid afternoon in the Meadowlands. Tommie Frazier had a great game, rushing for 130 yards on 12 carries and adding another 100 yards passing. We dominated the game with our defense shutting down their offense and won 31-0. West Virginia simply couldn't get anything going against us. Though we scored 31 points and moved the ball against a strong West Virginia defense, I felt our offensive execution was sloppy at times. We had five turnovers in the game, a couple of dropped passes and some missed blocking assignments.

Don Nehlen, the West Virginia coach, is a good friend and I felt badly for him after the game. He not only lost the game but his team suffered several critical injuries. Our game with West Virginia caused them to struggle through the first part of the season. However, they did recover to win several games toward the end of the year and became a good football team.

West Virginia's plight underscored one problem with an early game such as the Kickoff Classic. When two teams with good athletes and high aspirations play, the loser often loses confidence and momentum. Sometimes an injury or two will ruin a season before it even gets started. Playing an additional game such as this, while producing extra revenue, is a real gamble. In our case it worked out well since we received exposure on the east coast and made a good impression on national television.

With our victory over West Virginia, our ranking improved to No. 1 in both the AP and USA Today/CNN polls. It's better to be ranked No. 1 toward the end of the season than the beginning of the season. A top ranking late in the season assures that your team will play for the national title. The problem with being No. 1 early in the year is that you become a target. Every team you play wants to upset the highest ranked team in the country. However, I was sure that our team was mature enough to handle the situation, so I was confident that our high ranking was more positive than negative.

On September 8, we traveled to Lubbock to play Texas Tech. Tech is coached by Spike Dykes, another good friend. Spike has been in the game for a long time. He coached with Darrell Royal as an assistant at Texas when they had great football teams. Spike is at home in western Texas, as he is an easygoing, friendly individual who relates well to everyone.

We played well against Tech. Our rushing game was particularly outstanding. Tommie Frazier had another good game running the option and Lawrence Phillips rushed for 175 yards. In this game Lawrence carried the ball on my favorite play of the season—a simple dive play. Our offensive line knocked Tech's defensive line back 10 yards and walled off the safety man. This created a crease so large that Lawrence ran for a 56-yard touchdown. That touchdown was symbolic of how we played. We rushed for more than 500 yards and accumulated 600 yards of total offense. Although we played well defensively, Tech still made some big plays and scored 16 points. We won 42-16, and were also able to attract a national viewing audience on ESPN.

Unfortunately, we lost our starting safety, Mike Minter, to a season-ending injury. Mike called our defensive secondary signals and was an intelligent and gifted athlete. He fell and injured himself when he tackled a player as they were going out of bounds, resulting in a twisted and torn anterior cruciate ligament. Losing

Mike in the secondary was like losing a starting quarterback on offense. I was upset about losing him, but hoped he would successfully rehabilitate his knee before the end of the season. Without him in the lineup, we were very thin in the secondary.

Nine days later we played UCLA in Lincoln. This was our third consecutive game on television. We had another good offensive day. Our execution improved as we ran the football particularly well against the No. 13-ranked Bruins. We also took better care of the football and only turned over the ball once. Although we easily won the game, 49-21, I was disturbed that defensively we allowed UCLA to total more than 400 yards of offense. Still, we had come through three difficult games and were off to a great start.

I was worried about our passing game. We had thrown for 100 yards or less in all three games and our completion percentage was less than expected. Tommie Frazier had improved his throwing over the spring and summer, so we expected him to be at least a 55-60 percent passer. As always, Tommie's ability to run the ball was excellent. But I knew we needed to improve our passing game if we wanted to win the rest of our games.

As we prepared for our fourth game of the season against Pacific, Tommie began to complain of soreness in his leg. I really didn't think too much about his complaint. It wasn't until the morning of the game that I realized his injury might be serious. Tommie wasn't sure how long he could play before his leg would become too sore to move. We decided after talking to the doctors that he would start the game. If we gained control of the game, we planned to remove him immediately.

We had no business playing Pacific because we had a stronger program. But they were the only substitutes we could find when another team asked out of their contract. It's becoming more difficult to find teams to play in Lincoln without scheduling a return match at their stadium. The guarantee for coming to Lincoln, because of our large home attendance, is a significant payday for teams like Pacific. They needed the money and we needed the game. Unfortunately, it was one of those games you hate to play. You are expected to win—if you lose, it is perceived as the end of the world.

We wanted our players to give a great effort, but we didn't want to run up the score and embarrass Pacific. We played more than 100 players in the game. Pacific had some success throwing the ball, but the final score was 70-21.

Tommie Frazier was in the game for only nine plays. He did not sustain further injury but his leg was so sore we took him out. Brook Berringer came in and played most of the game. He completed 8 of 15 passes for 120 yards and three touchdowns. I did not know it at the time, but Tommie would not play again until the bowl game. The diagnosis following the game showed that he had a blood clot behind the right knee. He was admitted to the hospital and put on blood thinners in an attempt to dissolve the clot. Although his situation was not critical, it was serious. There was always some danger of the blood clot breaking loose and moving into the lungs, which could have been fatal. No one, including Tommie, knew what caused the clot to form.

I asked Dr. Deepak Gangahar to supervise Tommie's case. Dr. Gangahar had performed open heart surgery on me in 1984, and I had a great deal of confidence in his abilities. He said if the clot could be dissolved quickly, possibly Tommie could return to the football field before the end of the season. The clot could also reform or not completely dissolve.

I paid regular visits to Tommie in the hospital. On one visit I asked permission to pray with him. He said that would be fine. I wasn't sure where he was spiritually, but I believed it was appropriate to pray. Prayer is an important part of my life and I wanted Tommie to know that God cared for him, too. We prayed briefly and then I left. I didn't know exactly what effect Tommie's absence from our team would have on the rest of the season. There was no doubt that he was our key player. He had experience, confidence and ability. Many observers felt that without Tommie Frazier we would struggle and would probably lose several games.

Tommie had a great high school career while playing for Joe Kinnan at Manatee High School in Bradenton, Florida. Manatee High School had an excellent record under Joe, particularly with Tommie as quarterback. Tommie started his junior and senior years and went 19-1 in the regular season for those two years and 21-3 overall counting playoff games. When Tommie came to Nebraska, he was a very seasoned player, unlike most of the other freshmen. He had played under pressure, in big games and in front of large crowds. He was ready to start in a major college program as a freshman. Very few freshman players are as confident as he was, particularly at quarterback.

Tommie had been the subject of an intense recruiting struggle. It finally came down to Nebraska, Notre Dame and Clemson. All three schools ran some option football. When we recruited Tommie, we were not always at the top of his list. But he was sure at the top of our list! Kevin Steele, a former assistant coach, recruited in the southeastern part of the country and did a great job of recruiting Tommie. He developed a good relationship with Tommie's mother and father. Kevin, Tommie and his mother, Priscilla, played a lot of cards during the recruiting process. When Tommie came to Lincoln for his official visit, Kevin and I flew home with him, which was legal at the time. Unfortunately, I couldn't go to his house because I had already made my official visit. When we left to fly back to Lincoln, we had no idea whether or not he would choose Nebraska. But I never doubted he would be an important factor in the future of Nebraska football, if he would become a Cornhusker. Tommie committed to attend Nebraska a few days later. We were very pleased. I knew that his decision was a big plus for us, but I just didn't know how big.

When Tommie Frazier reported for practice in the fall of 1992, I was surprised at how quickly he learned the offense. He took notes in the meetings and obviously spent time in the evenings reviewing what we had gone over. Clearly, he had a sharp mind and a good memory; we seldom had to repeat anything to him. I was sure his confident attitude was developed during a successful high school career at Manatee. He also had an unshakable optimism that was probably developed during his formative years. His mother has a positive outlook and a ready smile, and I would imagine Tommie got his disposition from her.

Tommie was extremely quick. He had good speed, although not sprinters' speed. He had an exceptionally strong arm and large hands so he could grip the ball in almost any kind of weather condition. He was as good at ball handling and pitching the ball as any quarterback we have ever had. Tommie was not without some weaknesses, however. He lacked what coaches call "touch." He threw almost every pass with high velocity. There were times when it was difficult for him to ease off a throw that needed to be placed over linebackers or in a tight spot. He also needed to work on his footwork. Sometimes he threw the ball off balance, rather than stepping at the target. This is a common problem for quarterbacks with strong arms. They can throw off balance and still get the ball to their receiver, so they tend to depend on their arm strength too much. But accuracy begins to disintegrate as their footwork goes downhill. It was also tough for Tommie to admit to an error. Eventually, he got better at admitting his mistakes and learned from them as he developed into one of Nebraska's greatest quarterbacks.

Quarterback Coach Turner Gill and I thought he was making excellent progress for a freshman. However, in Tommie's mind, things weren't moving along fast enough. In fact, he thought he was ready to start after the third game. Turner, Kevin Steele and I visited with him. We were able to get him settled down and back on track. We convinced him that although he was an outstanding player, he wasn't ready to be thrown into the fire as the starter. A little bit of seasoning was still needed.

His first start came against Missouri in our sixth game of the season. He rushed 14 times for 77 yards and three touchdowns while he completed 9 of 20 passes for 157 yards. However, the most memorable game of his freshman season was a televised game against Colorado on Halloween night, 1992. Both teams were rated No. 8. Koy Detmer started for Colorado as a freshman quarterback and Tommie Frazier started for Nebraska, also as a freshman. Detmer had his first pass picked off and things just kept getting worse for Colorado. We won 52-7. It was a remarkable performance, and Tommie was a major factor in the win. It looked like we had become a great football team.

Only two weeks later, we were upset by Iowa State. With Tommie ailing from a slight knee strain, which he suffered early in the game, we were beaten 19-10. A combination of Tommie's injury, injuries to our two tight ends and a lack of emotional readiness led to a poor performance. Iowa State played a nearly flawless and emotional game. It turned out to be a tremendous disappointment as it took our momentum away toward the end of the season. Before the loss, we had been moving steadily upward in the rankings.

We did, however, win the Big Eight Championship by beating Oklahoma in Norman 33-9 in the final game of the season. Although we lost to Florida State 27-14 in the Orange Bowl, I was seeing signs that we were getting closer to competing with the best teams in the country. I thought Tommie's performance in that game was good considering we played an excellent Florida State team.

Florida State also had a great quarterback, Charlie Ward. If we had eliminated a couple of turnovers and a few mistakes in the kicking game, it would have been a close game. We finished the 1992 season 9-3 and Big Eight champs. Tommie had established himself as the first true freshman to play a significant role as the starting quarterback at Nebraska. We lost only one more game in which he started. That was the 18-16 loss to Florida State in the 1994 Orange Bowl.

While Tommie began to make his mark during the 1992 season, that year we also had a redshirt freshman quarterback, Brook Berringer, who saw little action. I noticed Brook at our football camp during the summer of 1990. Though he was from a small school in western Kansas, he impressed us with his maneuverability and throwing motion. Brook's high school career had been much different from Tommie's. Brook came from Goodland, Kansas and played at a school that didn't have great success in football. Brook was injured in his junior year and didn't play much but did well as a senior. Overall, the caliber of competition was not what Tommie had experienced at Manatee High School. Tommie was ready to make an immediate impact on our team because of his experience. Brook, on the other hand, developed more slowly and needed a redshirt year to develop his confidence and skills. I always felt Brook had the talent to be an outstanding quarterback at Nebraska. It was just going to take a little longer for him to develop his talent.

When Tommie entered the hospital with the blood clot problem, the burden to lead the team was placed squarely on Brook's shoulders. His first start came early in 1994 against Wyoming. We were heavily favored in the game, but Wyoming didn't seem to be aware of it. They had two coaches who had coached at Nebraska, Dave Butterfield and Scott Downing. I'm sure their involvement led to an emotionally charged Wyoming defense. While their defense had an outstanding first half, the offense also made a few big plays. They had us down 14-0 before the end of the first quarter, so we knew we were in a ballgame. Brook could have easily become rattled. Instead, he kept his focus and helped us win 42-32. Brook completed 15 of 22 passes with one interception. Our running game, as usual, was very strong. We had a significant statistical advantage over Wyoming. However, they did throw the ball effectively against us at times.

Near the end of the first half, on an 11-yard touchdown run, Brook took a hard hit to his back, just above his rib cage. He continued to play throughout the second half and made several big plays. I didn't realize how serious the injury was until the game was over. He complained of shortness of breath, so we had him X-rayed. The doctors found a collapsed lung and cracked ribs. Now we had a serious shortage of quarterbacks. Brook and Tommie were the only two scholarship quarterbacks on our team and they both had severe injuries.

Matt Turman came to Nebraska as a walk-on wide receiver from Wahoo, Nebraska. Since he played quarterback in high school and we needed more depth at quarterback, we asked Matt to move back to that position. Matt was 5-foot-10 and 170 pounds at the time, not as big as our quarterbacks usually are, but it looked like he would end up being a key player for us.

We only had one other quarterback, a freshman walk-on from Kearney, Nebraska, Monte Christo. We had already decided to redshirt him. Monte had torn a ligament in the thumb of his passing hand, so he had been sidelined for several weeks. During my coaching career at Nebraska, I could not remember being so thin at the quarterback position.

Tommie and Brook were both receiving treatment from Dr. Gangahar. A few days before the Oklahoma State game it was decided that Brook's lung was sufficiently healed for him to play. Everyone was nervous about Brook reinjuring himself, but he started the game and played well. Although Oklahoma State took a 3-0 lead, by halftime we regained the lead 9-3. Unfortunately, Brook was hit late in the second quarter and landed hard on his back. A halftime examination found that his lung had deflated again, so I looked over at Matt Turman and gave him the nod at quarterback.

We were down to our No. 3 quarterback, a walk-on, with nobody prepared to back him up if he was injured. Matt did a great job and we went on to win the game 31-3. I couldn't have been prouder of the way that he responded under very difficult circumstances. Matt is a distant relative by marriage. On that day, I was even more proud to claim Matt as a relative. It seemed that no matter what happened to this team, somebody was going to step forward and help us win. The defense seemed to realize that with the quarterback injuries, they needed to intensify their play. They played a great game against Oklahoma State, eliminating many big plays they gave up earlier in the year.

We were in serious trouble as we prepared to play Kansas State. They had gone from being a doormat in Division I college football to an outstanding football team under Coach Bill Snyder. Chad May, their quarterback, had hurt us by throwing for 489 yards in Lincoln the previous year. Dr. Gangahar told me that since Brook had collapsed a lung on successive weeks, he probably should not play against Kansas State. Matt would get the start while Brook would remain on the sidelines ready to play in an emergency. Dr. Deepak Gangahar is from India and had only witnessed American football from the stands. With Brook's injury, Deepak was on the sideline at the Oklahoma State game to monitor Brook's lung. He was surprised at the violent collisions created by the players. He turned to Pat Clare, one of our orthopedic surgeons and a former player at Nebraska, and mentioned that "these men are rather physical! I don't think they hesitate while taking a shot at you." I think Deepak was surprised at just how physical the game really is.

Matt started against Kansas State and played well in the first half. He took care of the football, but his height limited his down-field vision. A light rain was falling, which made it difficult for Matt to grip the football. His first warm-up throw before the game slipped out of his hand, so we knew we would have to lean primarily on our running game to carry the load. We ran the ball mostly between the tackles with Lawrence Phillips carrying. The Kansas State coaches realized we were committed to the run and overloaded the line of scrimmage with their defense.

We took a narrow lead, 7-6, into the half. In the locker room Dr. Gangahar suggested that perhaps Brook could play. Though he was a physician, he certainly wanted Nebraska to win. Brook did play in the second half, but we made sure he didn't run an option or throw a pass that allowed the defense to sack him. He didn't take a blow throughout the rest of the game. He complet-ed a pass to Abdul Muhammad in the fourth quarter that was a big play and set up a score. Jeff Makovicka, our fullback, made some big runs late in the game as well. Our defense played a superb game. Barron Miles, our cornerback, was simply out-standing as he broke up several passes. Our defense put enough pressure on Chad May that we only allowed Kansas State to score once. I was relieved when the game was over—we won 17-6.

We hadn't lost to Kansas State since a 12-0 loss in 1968. I still remember John Melton, our linebacker coach then, waiting with me in the press box until all the fans had left the stadium. Neither of us had ever seen such disappointed fans. We ended up 6-4 that year, and someone in Omaha was circulating a petition to fire Bob Devaney. Bob had turned the Nebraska program from obscurity to national prominence. The 12-0 loss in Lincoln was followed by an embarrassing loss to Oklahoma in one of the most lopsided games in Nebraska history. Our fans were really upset with us for playing so poorly. The experience taught me how quickly your fortunes can change in the football business. It was a sobering experience for me as a 32-year-old assistant coach. Fortunately, in 1994 we were able to escape with a win against Kansas State. I was tremendously proud of the tenacity with which our team played.

The next week we played an away game at Missouri. We weren't sure we could keep Brook from being reinjured against the Tigers. We thought if he went without injury to his lung in at least two consecutive games, he would be okay for the rest of the season. However, another injury to the lung might mean he would miss the rest of the season, and we planned to protect him as much as possible. Though we reduced the risks to Brook, he did throw the ball some. We stayed away from our option game most of the time. Again, both our offensive line and defense played a great game as we easily won.

The soap opera at quarterback continued when we replaced Brook late in the game with Matt Turman. Matt took a late hit out of bounds. It was obvious he was in a lot of pain, and it appeared he was hit on the point of his shoulder. A trainer reported to me that either he had a broken clavicle or a dislocated shoulder. I knew if that was true, he was lost for the rest of the season. That left us with either Brook or Monte Christo at quarterback. We wanted to preserve Monte's redshirt year, but I didn't want to risk putting Brook back in the game. Because it appeared that Matt would miss the rest of the season anyway, I decided to play Monte at quarterback. This would give Monte some needed experience to be our backup quarterback.

Monte was in for only a handful of plays as we drove the ball down the field at the end of the game. Following the game, X-rays and tests showed Matt Turman had only suffered a bruise to his shoulder. I was disappointed when I realized we might have wasted Monte's redshirt year by having him play for only a few minutes. We appealed the eligibility ruling to the Big Eight Conference and the NCAA. We wanted Monte to get an extra year of eligibility, but they denied our request because it was beyond the fifth game of the season. I felt badly about Monte losing a year of eligibility for such a short appearance in a game, but there was not anything else we could do to change the ruling.

The following week, we played Colorado in Lincoln. This was undoubtedly the biggest game of the season. Colorado had a great football team with several players who would later be high draft choices in the NFL. This game would not only decide the Big Eight Championship, but it would also play a role in the national championship picture. We had spent extra time preparing for Colorado during an open date earlier in the season. Our coaching staff tried to throw a few new wrinkles into our game plan.

Our plan seemed to work. We blitzed at the right time and kept Colorado's outstanding quarterback, Kordell Stewart, confused by our defensive strategy. Though Rashaan Salaam, the eventual Heisman Trophy winner, rushed for 134 yards, we held Colorado to only seven points.

Offensively, we controlled the ball and made big plays when they were needed. Brook had a great game and showed tremendous poise and confidence. He completed 12 of 17 passes for 142 yards and one touchdown. Our defense didn't allow Colorado a third- or fourth-down conversion during the whole game. Their only touchdown came late in the third quarter, when we were ahead 24-0. Neither team scored again, so the final score was 24-7. Our teams entered the game ranked No. 2 and No. 3, so most people expected a close game. In fact, many fans thought Colorado might have an edge because of Tommie's absence. By beating Colorado, we were ready to make a run at the national championship.

We beat Kansas the next week 45-17. Brook completed 13 of 18 passes for 267 yards and we had over 600 yards of total offense. The outcome was very different from the 21-20 win we had squeaked out the year before in Lawrence. That year we barely escaped a loss to Kansas when their two-point conversion failed late in the game.

Our next game was against Iowa State. We weren't nearly as sharp as we beat them 28-12. Brook threw a key touchdown pass to Abdul Muhammad late in the second quarter. The pass was perfect and the catch was one of the greatest catches I've ever seen. This play shifted the momentum toward us as we entered the second half. We scored twice in the fourth quarter to put the game away.

As we prepared for a game against our longtime rival Oklahoma, Tommie's return was a possibility. Even if he were only available as an emergency backup, his presence would provide a lift. Tommie had suffered a recurrence of the blood clot a week after being diagnosed with the original clot and returned to the hospital for a second time. Again, the blood clot was dissolved and minor surgery was done to tie off a small vein in his leg. Dr. Gangahar thought the vein was contributing to the blood clot problem. We originally didn't expect Tommie to return to play but became hopeful as his recovery was more rapid than anticipated. Dr. Gangahar took Tommie off blood thinners a few days before the Oklahoma game. This allowed him to play against Oklahoma if we needed to use him as a backup.

I'm sure it was difficult for Tommie to sit on the sidelines for the nine weeks he was injured. He had been the most publicized player on our team and suddenly he faded into the background as Brook led the team. Tommie never said too much and stayed positive, but it must have bothered him. I'm sure his injury taught him a lesson about how quickly sports fame can vanish. In sports, you're a hero one day and forgotten the next. All it takes is a freak accident, like Tommie's, for the attention of the fans to be shifted to the next player in the spotlight.

Although Oklahoma didn't have a great record, I was anxious about the game because they always have lots of talent. Gary Gibbs was a sound coach who understood our system and always had his team ready to play us—particularly on defense. If their quarterbacks had played more consistently during the season, I'm sure they would have won several more games.

As I expected, they played a great game on defense, especially against the run. We had some success throwing the ball and were able to shut down their offense. We didn't score much, so it's a good thing we had a great defensive game. Eventually, Brook threw a key pass to Abdul Muhammad, which set up the final score as we won 13-3. It was our second consecutive undefeated regular season. We held Oklahoma to only 179 yards of total offense and intercepted two passes. Although Tommie was suited up on the sideline, we didn't use him in the game. A few fans speculated that Brook was not as effective because Tommie was there and able to play. To the contrary, Brook showed a lot of poise and played a fine game. I credit the Oklahoma defense for keeping us from scoring more.

3

SUCCESS IN MIAMI—FINALLY!

With only five weeks until the bowl game, we were faced with a dilemma. Tommie would likely be cleared to play in the bowl game, so everyone was curious about whom we would choose to start at quarterback. We decided to do what we've always done—start the player who had the best performance in practice and scrimmages. No matter which player started, we planned to play both quarterbacks at least some of the game. We felt both quarterbacks deserved a chance to contribute in the bowl game because we needed both to win during the season. Many fans didn't understand why we would give Tommie a chance to win his starting job back, after Brook had successfully led our team to seven consecutive wins. For Tommie, however, there was never a time when he wasn't successful as our quarterback. We felt it was only fair to let them compete for the starting position on the field. Both Brook and Tommie practiced well, but in the final scrimmage before the bowl, Brook didn't play as well as Tommie. He had more turnovers in the scrimmage so we gave the starting nod to Tommie.

As the season unfolded, we had risen to a No. 1 ranking. Undefeated Penn State was ranked No. 2. Penn State had just joined the Big Ten Conference, so, as Big Ten Champions, they were obligated to play in the Rose Bowl. As Big Eight Champions we were bound to the Orange Bowl; therefore, there was no way we could play Penn State for the national championship. Instead, we played the University of Miami in the Orange Bowl for the third time in seven years. I felt it was a stroke of bad luck.

Howard Schnellenberger, a former Miami coach, said the University of Miami's home-field advantage was worth about 10 points. Based upon my experience with Miami—I agreed with him. During midwinter in Nebraska, the humidity is very low, so when we travel to Miami it's like practicing in a steam bath. Temperature is not the problem, but the humidity is, and you only have about a week to adjust to the change in climate. We always tried to compensate for the change with a lot of extra conditioning.

The noise factor in the Orange Bowl is another problem. We prepared for the crowd noise by simulating it with huge stereo speakers blasting out music or crowd noise during our practices. By simulating the crowd noise, our players could make their adjustments for the game with hand signals or by shouting.

Personally, I felt the most difficult challenge was playing Miami's top-ranked defense. Miami was ranked No. 3 in the polls and had lost only to Washington, their only loss in more than 60 home games. The combination of Miami's tremendous talent and home-field advantage made them nearly unbeatable. The Miami mystique was much more than good press. They were for real! I was willing to play Penn State anywhere. I even told our athletic director I wanted to propose a coin flip to decide which bowl would host a game between the No. 1 and No. 2 teams. Of course, that was only wishful thinking since both the Orange and Rose Bowls had ironclad contracts with each team. I knew my suggestion would only cause more controversy. Yet, I wonder if both bowls wouldn't have liked at least a chance to host a true national championship game.

Although I wasn't very excited about playing Miami with their home-field advantage, I knew that a win against them would help make up for previous disappointing losses to them in the Orange Bowl. I also knew that a win over Miami, in Miami, would quite likely give us a national championship, no matter what Penn State did against Oregon in the Rose Bowl.

It still hurts to think about the disappointing loss to Miami in 1984. We lost 31-30 after we came back from an early 17-0 deficit. Few Husker fans have forgotten the missed two-point conversion toward the end of the game, which cost us the national championship. We were also humiliated in 1989, when we lost 23-3 to a second-ranked Miami team. The 1992 Orange Bowl game against Miami was a particularly bitter pill to swallow as we failed to score and got beat 22-0. It was the first game in which we had been shut out in 221 games going back to the 1973 season. Jimmy Johnson won the national championship that night. I can still picture the Miami players carrying Jimmy around the field after they won the game as Jimmy put on quite an emotional display. In short, our memories about playing Miami were not good ones.

We knew this Miami team could just as easily break our hearts as past teams had done. Although their offense was a little weaker than some previous Miami teams, their defense was possibly better than any of their national championship teams. Fortunately for us, our team played the season with tremendous tenacity and determination to win. Our players were committed to completing their goal of winning the national championship. The near-upset of Florida State the year before led to a highly motivated group of players who would not be denied a national title for the second time.

I had never seen a team pull together against all odds to win like this team. When the offense was struggling, our defense stopped our opponent's offense. When the defense had trouble, we simply outscored the other team. And through it all, our kicking game remained rock solid. Darin Erstad was an outstanding baseball player for Nebraska, so when he joined the football team as a kicker, we knew he was a great athlete. However, once we placed him on a football scholarship, we saw just how much we had been missing. Darin became a great punter and was our long-range field-goal kicker. He could kick 60-yard field goals with some regularity and kicked off into the end zone consistently. Tom Sieler, a 5th-year walk-on player from Nevada, was our place-kicker for shorter field goals and points after touchdowns.

As we prepared for the game, we never forgot Miami's winning streak at home. They had won 62 of the last 63 games at home. They were ranked No. 1 in total defense, pass defense and scoring defense. Their rushing defense was also ranked No. 7. We were leading the nation in rushing, so something was going to give. Our defense was ranked in the top 10 in every category and we were second to Miami in scoring defense. I was sure it would be a low scoring game, which would be decided in the fourth quarter. If there was a phase of the game where we were stronger, it had to be the kicking game.

Our coaching staff was convinced we could wear them down by the fourth quarter. Our confident attitude wasn't simply wishful thinking. I knew the odds were not in our favor, but our strength and depth on both sides of the football could help us overcome Miami's strengths. We planned to rotate our players, particularly our defensive linemen, and hoped that they could generate a good pass rush throughout the game. Often a pass rush is ineffective late in a game against a team that throws the ball 50 to 60 times a game. It takes much more energy for a defensive player to rush a passer than for an offensive lineman to protect the quarterback. Unless you rotate those pass rushers against a passing team in Miami's humidity, you are asking for trouble.

Miami took a 10-0 lead in the first quarter. They intercepted the football on their 3-yard line when Tommie was hit as he released the ball. Then they drove down the field and scored on a 34-yard pass from Frank Costa to Trent Jones. I'm sure many fans counted us out once Miami took a 10-0 lead. Because of their great defense, their lead seemed nearly insurmountable.

We put Brook in the game during the second quarter, and he led our team on our first sustained drive. Brook completed the drive by throwing a 19-yard touchdown pass to our tight end, Mark Gilman. With Mark's score we only trailed 10-7 at halftime. I felt Miami's defense was beginning to tire as we took control of the line of scrimmage toward the end of the half.

Unfortunately, I knew Miami would have plenty of time to recover during the halftime break. The Orange Bowl is known for its halftime pageantry, and their halftimes generally run much longer than the regulation 20 minutes. After the half, Miami took the ball down the field as Costa completed a 44-yard pass to Jonathan Harris to put Miami up by 10 points with less than two minutes gone in the third quarter. I reminded the players of our goals for the game during the half. These goals were to avoid unnecessary penalties, continue to play hard, avoid taunting and to keep the pressure on their quarterback. I told them we would win if we continued to do these four basic things. Normally, I don't predict a victory, but I felt confident in our ability to win the game in the fourth quarter.

Our players continued to put together a team effort as the second half ticked away. Our defense began to dominate the line of scrimmage. Dwayne Harris sacked Costa for a safety, which made the score 17-9. We didn't move the ball during the next series, but we gained field position when Darin Erstad hit a booming punt.

Finally, we got the big break we were waiting for when Miami's center snapped the ball over the punter's head on the first drive of the fourth quarter. This turnover gave us the ball on their 4-yard line. On first down, Brook threw the ball under pressure and was intercepted by a Miami defender in the corner of the end zone. Because he was forced to throw off his back foot, he didn't get enough zip on the football to throw it out of the end zone, as his receiver was covered.

The turnover was a real setback to our team. We had finally started to control the game, much as we did toward the end of the second half. The momentum seemed to shift to our team as Miami's defense had worn down during the second half. Suddenly, after the interception, they had the ball on the 20-yard line, and we had blown a chance to score. We drill our players to avoid turnovers inside the opponent's 20-yard line. If we don't score a touchdown, we at least need to get a shot at a field goal. I was frustrated and was afraid we were letting the game slip away. But our team never gave up. They didn't allow the circumstances to affect their attitude. In fact, Miami never crossed the 50-yard line again as we began to dominate the game.

Warren Sapp was a great defensive player for Miami who helped their defense dominate opponents throughout the season. Once during the fourth quarter, Sapp gave me a long look and gestured toward me as he chased a running back near the sideline. I'm not sure what he meant by the gesture, but it was obvious he wanted me to see it. Sapp and the rest of his teammates spent less time talking and taunting as we started to control the ball.

We put Tommie back in the game at the start of the fourth quarter. Brook had played about half the game and I felt it was time to give Tommie a chance to lead the team. I knew some fans would second-guess my decision to replace Brook, but I thought we needed a change of pace. It was time to run some option football. Tommie was rested and eager to get in the game. Darin Erstad made another great punt and the ball went dead at the Miami 4-yard line. Our defense held and we got the ball back in great field position with 8:11 left on the clock. Lawrence Phillips ran for 25 yards, the longest running play against the Miami defense for the entire season. On the next play, fullback Cory Schlesinger broke a trap play over the right side for a 15-yard touchdown. The play seemed to confuse the Miami defense. We used a blocking scheme that we hadn't used previously during the season. Although Cory made a great run, the offensive line opened a nice hole for him.

At this point the score was 17-15, so we went for a two-point conversion. Tommie completed a pass to tight end Eric Alford on a bootleg. The corner of the end zone where he caught the pass was poorly lighted, so I couldn't tell if Eric scored. Tommie always throws the ball hard and this pass was no exception. But Eric hung on to the pass, so we tied the game. The two-point conversion was symbolic, since it was another play-action pass in the same corner of the end zone where we had failed on the two-point play against Miami in the 1984 Orange Bowl.

Our defense stopped Miami on the next series of downs, and after the ensuing punt, we took over on our own 42-yard line with 6:22 left in the game. We lost a yard on first down, and then Tommie completed a 7-yard pass to Reggie Baul. This brought up a critical third down. We needed to gain four yards for the first down. We were at the 48-yard line, so I decided to let Tommie make a play. He generally made the big plays when we needed them, so I was confident he could do it again. Tommie ran an option to the right side and kept the ball for a terrific 25-yard run. That play put us at their 27-yard line. Lawrence Phillips gained seven yards on the next play. Then Tommie ran an option for a 6-yard gain.

On first down, I called another trap play. I told the ball carrier to instruct our left guard, Brendan Stai, to add emphasis to his false block. I wanted him to show pass, so Warren Sapp would move upfield which would allow Brendan to slip inside the defense to block their linebacker. This allowed our right guard Joel Wilks to trap Sapp while Cory Schlesinger ran up the middle. Sapp was coming so hard that the false block worked perfectly and Joel didn't need to throw a block on Sapp. The middle linebacker was blocked by Brendan, and Cory broke to the left and ran between the two safeties and dove into the end zone to give us the lead 23-17.

Miami was completely worn down at this point. They were having trouble protecting Costa. Both our offensive and defensive lines were in control. Miami took over the ball with 2:46 remaining. Costa was sacked twice—once by Terry Connealy and once by Dwayne Harris. Then on fourth down Costa went deep, and Kareem Moss, our strong safety, intercepted the pass. Tommie knelt down for two plays as the clock ran out, and we had finally reached our goal after 23 years. This win was especially sweet as we had come so close and yet failed to win the national championship in the 1984 and 1994 Orange Bowl games.

In retrospect, the law of averages probably should have allowed us to win one of those two, if not both. However, I felt fortunate at that moment to have been part of a team that showed so much heart and character. They had dealt with adversity most of the season, yet they never lost sight of our goals. I was elated with the win, but wasn't any more proud of our football team than I had been the year before when we had come up short against Florida State. In both games, our players displayed the hearts of champions.

The scene in the locker room after the game was highly emotional because our team had overcome many obstacles and had grown close. I believe there was about as much genuine warmth and caring between players and coaches as I had ever seen. We had our traditional silent postgame prayer and then everybody cut loose; there were lots of hugs and a few moist eyes. I left the locker room and headed for the press interview and ran into my wife. Nancy was really excited to see me and her entire face glowed. I knew the victory meant as much to her as it did to me. The Nebraska fans were great and waited around for more than an hour after the game. Many players and coaches came out of the dressing room and waved and saluted the fans. It was gratifying to have close to 20,000 fans stay after the game to celebrate with us.

When we returned to Lincoln the next day, I was moved by the thousands of fans who stood next to the road as we drove from the airport to the Devaney Center to celebrate our championship. It was a typical midwinter Nebraska day. It was cold and most of the fans were standing in snow as they cheered wildly for our team. I don't think I realized how much the Nebraska fans had wanted to win a national championship. I appreciated their loyalty to our team.

The Devaney Center basketball arena was jammed with over 15,000 fans. Several university and state officials made comments, as did some players. I regret having our assistant coaches stand below us on the ground level of the Devaney Center. It was unfortunate to have them receive so little of the credit for our success. We have, in my estimation, the best group of assistants in the country. Their experience and loyalty to the program is unmatched. It's too bad that I usually get so much credit when we do well. We all share equally when we win or lose. Our staff and players deserve more credit for our success.

A few days later I was named the National Coach of the Year by the American Football Coaches Association. This was a real tribute to our entire staff and organization as it is recognition of a coaching job by an entire staff. The assistant coaches do 90 percent of the coaching and recruiting, so the honor represents their efforts as much as mine.

My only regret about receiving the award was that Bob Devaney didn't receive the same award. There is no doubt in my mind that he is the most deserving coach who never received the award in college football history. In 1970 and 1971, when we won our first two national championships, the coach of the year balloting was done before the bowl games. Therefore, he didn't receive the award though we won national championships in both years. In 1971, we beat Paul Bryant's Alabama team 38-6. Paul was named Coach of the Year before the bowl game. Obviously, because of the way things turned out, Bob was the more deserving coach. I know it has always bothered him that he didn't receive the award. I would gladly have given him mine.

The months following our national championship were wonderful. When we visited the White House, President Clinton graciously spent time with our entire team. Everyone seemed to love us. Even the national press was impressed with our season. Things were going almost too smoothly. I told Nancy that the smooth ride couldn't last—it certainly didn't.

4

THE MISSION

As we began preparation for the 1995 season, we knew our players couldn't rely on their unfulfilled dreams to motivate them as they had the previous year. We had lost the national championship the year before after a narrow 18-16 loss to Florida State in the 1994 Orange Bowl. Following that disappointing loss, Boyd Epley, our strength and conditioning coach, had 1:16 put on our stadium scoreboard clock. It had served as a poignant reminder during our team's summer workouts of how close we came to beating Florida State. The players were determined to not let up in their pursuit of the national championship. I've coached few teams that showed so much enthusiasm toward reaching their goal.

Many championship teams have turned in mediocre encores. It's easy to become complacent and lose focus once you've reached the pinnacle of success. I was concerned about a letdown as we began preparation for the 1995 season. Contrary to what many people think, football teams don't prepare for their season just a few weeks before kickoff. Instead, it begins in January following the preceding season. Our winter conditioning runs from the third week of January through the second week of March. It involves heavy lifting, agility work, speed work and skill and technique drills as well. In 1995, our players worked hard during this phase of their preparation and continued to have the same intensity and commitment they had the year before.

Spring football follows the seven weeks of winter conditioning. We are only allowed 10 practices with full pads out of 15 total practices. Although we have fewer practices in pads, it doesn't lessen the value of spring ball. We still use this time to teach the players fundamentals and allow them to compete for a spot on the depth chart.

The major concern we had going into spring football was the replacement of four starters on the offensive line. Three of the linemen we lost were drafted into the National Football League and started several games as rookies. It seemed like an impossible task to replace the "pipeline" which included Rob Zatechka, Brendan Stai, Zach Wiegert and Joel Wilks. It was a nice surprise during spring ball when several of our offensive linemen, who saw limited playing time the year before, stepped up their play against our defense. I knew if our offensive line could play well against our defense, we could move the football on any team in the country. Though both the defense and offense were extremely aggressive during our scrimmages, we suffered few injuries during spring ball.

Their excellent work continued into the summer. Many players stayed in Lincoln during the summer so they could use our training facilities. It was common for them to attend summer school in the mornings, have part-time jobs in the afternoons and still find time to work out in the evenings. Although the workouts were unsupervised by our coaches, I could tell from talking with the players that they were focused on the right things. Everything pointed toward another run at the national championship.

We had lost seven offensive and seven defensive starters from the 1994 national championship team. We also lost our punter and place-kickers to graduation. On paper, we had few reasons to be optimistic. But after seeing their work ethic during the spring and summer, my confidence in our team had grown. I felt they could be a much better team than I had first thought.

The first thing we did at our initial staff meeting in early August was to develop what many organizations call a mission statement. The statement we developed said:

- Be hard working, thorough, professional and loyal.
- Maximize each player's character and talent.
- Operate with integrity.
- Promote unity, pride and confidence in the team.
- Promote the value of education.
- Treat everyone with respect.

Our staff spends several hours each year developing this mission statement. It gives us direction for the season. Each year we try to take a fresh look at our mission. Although there are often similarities from previous years, there are always a few changes. We try hard to make our mission statement relevant to each team. It's easy to let any mission statement become simply words on a plaque or poster. We hang the mission statement in our staff meeting room so it's a constant reminder of our purpose. As the season unfolds, I ask the entire staff to evaluate our team based on our mission statement.

Our coaching staff is firmly convinced that each of them needs to agree to a common set of standards. I believe many organizations get in trouble at this point. If you assume incorrectly that your group is unified when they are not, you will be headed in different directions. For example, if your mission statement stresses you should treat each member of your team with respect and positive support, yet key members of the group use threats and humiliation to achieve their goals—you might as well scrap your mission statement.

Here is a summary, line-by-line, of what we established as our goals for the 1995 season. The mission statement begins by declaring the necessity of a strong work ethic. When we began meeting in August, each of us knew we were facing six months of long hours. We spend seven days a week, an average of 12 to 14 hours a day—sometimes even longer, working toward our goal. Nebraska fans eagerly await football to begin during the spring and summer. But most of our coaches are not nearly as enthusiastic about the beginning of the season. We look forward to the season, but we often dread the mental and physical demands each season requires. College football pushes every coach to his limit. There are no breaks, no reprieves and no second chances.

The mission statement also challenges us to be thorough. It is so easy to become complacent and not spend enough time reviewing film or missing a personnel change that an opponent has made or overlooking a detail in the kicking game. We prepare for each game with the same methodical and meticulous approach. Every possible strategy is considered. Coaches don't want surprises during a game. And while we know it's impossible to prepare for every move, we also know that successful teams pay attention to the details.

Recruiting requires this same thoroughness. Before we offer a scholarship, we look at several of the recruit's game tapes, check his academic status, and talk with his coaches, teachers and counselors about his attitude and character. It's important for us to evaluate how each recruit might fit into our program. Again, attention to detail is critical when we judge any recruit.

We also try to be professional. Quite often people refer to the coaching "profession," and yet, some people think it's anything but professional. This negative attitude probably results from the few coaches who abuse their relationships with athletes. I've known coaches who lash out at a recruit for not choosing to attend their school. Coaches can take out their frustration on a player when he repeatedly blows his assignments. Any coach who lacks self-control only serves to diminish his profession in the eyes of the public. Although the demands on any college coach are great, we expect our staff to conduct themselves as professionals in every area of coaching. If we want to be treated like "professionals" then we need to act like professionals.

We also put a premium on loyalty. I believe loyalty begins with the head coach setting the example. If the head coach models loyalty to his staff and players—hopefully, they will reciprocate. If you show genuine concern and support for your players, you can count on them returning your support—even when the heat is on.

Maximizing each player's character and talent is the second premise of the mission statement. We believe that each player has certain unique gifts. Some may have more talent than others, but each player has traits that are important. Our goal is to develop each player's athletic, academic, social and spiritual gifts. It's more likely that their talents will be maximized when they feel secure in their relationship with their coach. Any player who thinks he is only a means to an end or a pawn in a chess game, will undoubtedly crumble emotionally under the intense pressure and scrutiny he faces as a college athlete. A kind word or gesture goes a long way toward helping an athlete know he is valued for who he is and not just for what he does on the football field.

Integrity is the third and perhaps most important theme in our mission statement. The NCAA has plenty of rules and we expect our coaches and players to follow all of them. We teach our players to be honest and to keep their commitments. Again, we ask our coaches to model the behavior we expect from our players. We need to be honest with our players if we expect them to keep their promises. It's easy to tell a player what he wants to hear when you are recruiting him. But we believe the truth is the right approach—even if it means losing a highly sought-after recruit. In the long haul, being ethical serves any program well.

The fourth theme in our mission statement relates to teamwork. Our goal is to promote unity, pride and confidence in the team. This can only happen when our coaching staff uses constructive criticism, rather than undermining the confidence of the players. Each coach exercises much influence over his players. Whatever he says, negative or positive, has a much greater impact on a young person than he often realizes. Because of the coach's position of authority, he needs to be careful not to abuse his position. It's easy for a young person to let negative feedback affect him. This can be a problem in college, but it can be a bigger problem in high school or junior high. A more mature athlete is less likely to internalize negative feedback than the less mature athlete. I can assure you from personal experience, however, that even a mature professional athlete can be destroyed by his coach's negativism.

We do everything possible to create an environment that will promote unity. The more our players care, understand, and share a common purpose, the stronger the team. It's also important to affirm the players with encouraging words and gestures. Hopefully, with the proper support, they will develop a sense of confidence as a team. The support must be genuine and realistic. Otherwise, the words of encouragement will be seen as phony. To me, coaching consists of catching a player doing something right and reinforcing that behavior. There are times when correction is necessary, but constantly nagging a player for their miscues is only counterproductive. So many coaches see "coaching" as telling players what they are doing wrong. Telling them they are doing something right is even more important.

Education is the next theme in our mission statement. We believe in the value of education. The importance of education is constantly preached to our players. Without a college degree most college athletes will not be successful. Professional teams offer large amounts of money to any athlete who can make their team. Unfortunately, too many athletes attend college with the idea that success is signing a large professional contract.

According to the National Football League Players Association, the average professional player has a career of only 3.1 years. Over 50 percent of the players leaving the National

Football League leave without any financial resources. Of course, only a very small percentage of major college athletes ever make a professional football team.

Even if a player is fortunate enough to play a few years in the National Football League and make a lot of money, he will still have 30 to 40 productive years left once his career is over. I have seen many cases where a former professional athlete struggles to find fulfillment once he retires from football. Lack of education is usually the reason so many former pros fail to reach their goals after football.

Johnny Rodgers won the Heisman Trophy in 1972 and was one of the most talented athletes I have ever seen. Yet at age 42, Johnny came back to the University of Nebraska to complete his undergraduate degree. Johnny had intelligence, energy, recognition and owned his own business in San Diego. But without an education even Johnny found it difficult to reach his goals. If there was ever a football player who had a chance to be successful without a college degree—it was Johnny. His charisma and ambition set him apart from others. I admire him for returning to school so he can complete his degree after being out of school for over 20 years.

The final component of our mission statement is to treat others with respect. It is important for coaches to treat fellow coaches and players with respect. It is also important for players to treat others with respect. We live in a society where lack of civility is commonplace. There is no excuse for bad manners, yet we find that many young men come into our program without a basic understanding of common civility. Again, this is an area where we as coaches try to teach by example and encourage the players to practice these skills off the field.

5

EARLY TROUBLE

On August 2, 1995, I received a phone call that was to set the tone for the season. A local attorney called to notify us that there was a warrant out for the arrest of one of our players, Riley Washington. Immediately I called the County Attorney, Gary Lacey, to confirm the local attorney's story. Lacey told me that they had issued a warrant for the arrest of a football player named Washington.

When informed about the warrant, Riley appeared totally surprised that he was charged with anything. He didn't act like someone who had committed a crime the night before. He spent the morning in class and in our academic center studying. I told Riley he needed an attorney because he was charged with attempted murder. However, I explained I couldn't advise him about which attorney to select because that would violate NCAA rules. All I could do was to give him a phone book and let him pick his own attorney from the yellow pages. The first attorney

Riley picked was a name he recognized. Unfortunately, that attorney was out playing golf, so he picked another name at random. The second attorney he called agreed to escort him to police headquarters. Riley had already decided to turn himself in rather than be arrested later that night.

I didn't question Riley about the shooting. I had been warned that I could be subpoenaed and possibly accused of having coached Riley on what he should do or say regarding the shooting if I questioned him at length before he had turned himself in.

Later that night, Riley was booked and jailed. I couldn't call his parents because their phone had been disconnected. Finally, around 11:30 p.m. I got a call from his mother who had been told by a relative that Riley was in trouble. It wasn't easy trying to inform and comfort his mother. She was understandably upset and confused by the news that her son was charged with attempted murder. We both believed Riley was a good person, so it was hard to imagine him doing anything that terrible.

Two other individuals, Abdul Muhammad and Willis Brown, were with Riley the night of the shooting. Both Abdul and Willis were former Nebraska football players. Abdul had played for us for the previous four years and Willis had played one year before a career-ending injury.

According to Willis, early in the evening on August 1, he and Riley saw several people with whom they had had trouble from time to time at a store. One young man, Jermaine Cole, allegedly threatened both Riley and Willis. Since they wanted to avoid trouble, they jumped in their car and left.

Later that evening, Abdul, Willis and Riley went to a Kwik Shop. They soon noticed several cars gathering outside. When

Abdul and Willis left the store, Cole confronted them. According to Abdul and Willis, he jumped in front of them, took his shirt off and challenged them to a fight. Abdul admitted that he threw the first punch. Riley later told me he saw the fight as he left the Kwik Shop. A few moments later he heard shots. Everyone scattered when they heard the shots. Riley and Willis ran side by side with Abdul trailing them by about 50 feet. Eventually, they ran to a neighbor's home.

Riley was told the next day he was charged with attempted murder. He was accused of shooting Cole, who had confronted the players twice during the evening. Cole was shot in his side. Cole blamed Riley for the shooting. The police then issued a warrant for Riley's arrest. Cole and his friend, Alec Hogan, both implicated Riley. Each of them had been arrested numerous times. Cole had also been charged with giving false information to the police on several other occasions.

No test was given to Riley that would have indicated whether or not he had recently fired a gun when he checked into the jail at 5 p.m. on August 2. A test could have been helpful in determining Riley's innocence or guilt. I've been told that any person who discharges a weapon within 24 hours can be tested for traces of gun powder from the firearm. Riley's bond was set at $100,000, making it very difficult for Riley to get out on bail since his family couldn't pay the $10,000 needed to post bail on a $100,000 bond. Riley's mother had lost her job, so she could neither post the bond nor fly from her home in San Diego to Lincoln.

We hoped Riley could get out of jail so he could finish his summer school classes. According to NCAA rules, no members of the coaching staff or any representative of university athletic interest could post his bond. Therefore, we weren't sure how Riley could raise the $10,000 bail.

Because of Riley's mother's disconnected phone, I was forced to call a family friend who lived near her whenever I wanted to contact her about Riley. She would wait for my call at a pre-arranged time. Riley's mother assured me that she knew that I would stand by Riley and would do what I could to help him.

Riley's arrest confused and worried his family and friends. He was a mild-mannered young man with a good reputation. His friends in Lincoln had never known him to carry a gun, and no one believed that he could shoot someone. I felt sorry for Riley's family because they were hearing reports in San Diego that Riley had been dismissed from school for murdering someone. Of course, the false reports only made it more difficult for Riley's mother to deal with her son's problem.

The local media covered Riley's story to the hilt. A young man named Konji Mason gave a graphic description on television of Riley shooting Cole. Riley told me Mason was not even present at the shooting scene, something Mason later admitted. Riley was given a huge dose of negative publicity, much of it inaccurate. And while the rest of his teammates prepared for the season, Riley could only stare at the walls of his jail cell.

Riley stayed in jail for 13 days. During this period I visited him 10 times. The only days I didn't visit him were days when our practices interfered with his visitation times. During the first few days Riley was in jail, he was fairly upbeat and positive. But as each day passed, he became more depressed and discouraged. I felt he was frustrated that no one had stepped forward to post his bond. I'm sure the seriousness of his situation was also becoming more clear with each passing day. I was also sure he must have wondered if he would ever get out jail. Several times, I asked him point blank if he shot the gun. Each time he denied shooting Cole and said he was being falsely accused. Riley's story never changed. He always maintained his innocence.

Usually, a player will tell me the truth if I spend enough time with him. There is generally a strong mutual trust and respect between our coaches and players. Riley never wavered from his original story and as time went on, I began to believe him more and more.

After the first few days of confinement, it became obvious he wouldn't be able to complete his summer school class. It wasn't possible to take his final exam or even to give him his school books. The jail policy wouldn't allow any books to be brought to inmates. Apparently, they feared someone from the outside would smuggle narcotics into prison by putting the drugs between the book pages. Their policy appeared too strict to me, especially because we were only trying to help Riley complete his college degree. He was so close to completing his summer school course and I hated to see him fail.

They kept Riley in solitary confinement because they feared another inmate would attempt to harm him. I knew Riley wasn't worried about anybody, but I suspected the authorities wanted to protect him from other inmates who may have been friends of Cole. Each day he was in solitary confinement wore him down more. He wasn't allowed any television or much reading material. He spent most of his day staring at the walls of his cell. Occasionally, a visitor would break up the monotony.

As I thought about Riley's predicament, I was reminded of the thousands of people who are serving time in prison. When I've volunteered time for prison ministries, I've met many kind and thoughtful prisoners. Most of them never thought they would find themselves behind prison bars. It may only take an emotional outburst or an unusual set of circumstances for any of us to find ourselves behind bars. Many prisoners go day after day, month after month, and year after year with practically no support from the outside world. I'm reminded of Jesus' comments in the book of Matthew, "For I was hungry and you gave me something to eat, I was thirsty and you gave me something to drink, I was a stranger and you invited me in, I needed clothes and you clothed me, I was sick and you looked after me, I was in prison and you came to visit me." I'm not a religious fanatic and I'm not soft on crime. Many of our nation's prisoners are dangerous and need to be incarcerated. But there are also some decent people behind bars. I've met some of them.

Finally, someone who had employed Riley during the summer stepped forward to help him. He wanted to get together several people he knew to post Riley's bail. Unfortunately, once his friends discovered it was Riley who needed the bail money, they backed down from helping him. Few people in Lincoln believed Riley was innocent. Therefore, it was nearly impossible to find anyone who was willing to help bail him out.

Eventually, Jacques Allen's father came forward and posted half the bail money. Jacques played on our team, so his father Jerry knew Riley and liked him. Riley's girlfriend's family posted the other half of the bail. In neither case were these people representatives of university athletic interests, so there was no violation of NCAA rules.

One pleasant surprise took place just before Riley's release from jail. Some Texas friends of Riley's mother collected enough money to pay for half of his bail. They reimbursed Jerry Allen for his share of the bail money.

When the football team heard Riley was having trouble raising his bail, the players responded by offering to raise the money themselves. The captains told me the team met and were willing to sacrifice their monthly scholarship check to post Riley's bail. They each receive $190 per month for room and board. I was moved by their willingness to help Riley. It also indicated to me that his teammates didn't think that Riley was the type of person who would do what he was charged with. I know Riley was surprised and deeply appreciated his teammates' gesture. However, this, too, would have been an NCAA violation.

Riley was finally released from jail on August 15. Now the problem was whether I should let him play football. Most people seemed convinced of Riley's guilt. But each day I was becoming more convinced that he was innocent. It was clear from talking with the Public Defender's office that his case wouldn't be brought to trial for more than six months. There was only a slim chance that his case would be dropped after the preliminary hearing. It looked like Riley would either miss the entire season or I would have to reinstate him. I knew our entire program would be criticized if I let him play before he was found not guilty by the legal system. I also knew that I would not feel right about further penalizing and humiliating someone whom I believed had been wrongfully charged.

Riley's case will be decided by a jury in the summer of 1996. It is difficult to predict how a jury will perceive the evidence. I believe he is innocent because he has always told me the truth. There is a risk in becoming emotionally attached to your players. It is possible that my relationship with him could cloud my judgment, but I don't think that's the case. As John Wooden, the former UCLA basketball coach, writes in his book *They Call Me Coach*, "I often tell my players that next to my own flesh and blood, they are the closest to me. They are my children. I get wrapped up in them, their lives and their problems."

I try to be fair and give each player the treatment he earns and deserves; however, it is difficult to be entirely dispassionate and even-handed when dealing with those you care about.

6

A GOOD START

The day after Riley Washington's arrest our freshmen reported for their physicals. This was the most impressive group of freshmen I had seen in 33 years as a coach at Nebraska. Their size and strength were outstanding. And nearly every freshman was a highly sought-after recruit. These guys definitely looked like college football players.

After the physical exams, we put them through a series of tests that assess speed, explosiveness, agility and endurance. Our coaching staff joined the freshmen once the tests began. When we evaluated our freshmen, we discovered that although they had good speed and explosion, they were out of shape.

Our best indicator of physical conditioning is the 300-yard shuttle run, a very fatiguing test. The freshmen run twice with five minutes of rest between runs. We then take the average time for the two shuttle runs. We have a cutoff time that each position on the football team needs to meet. The linemen have the slowest standard, the linebackers and tight ends are next slowest, and the fastest time is required of the backs and receivers. Ten of the 22 freshmen tested did not make the necessary 300-yard shuttle run standard. Those who didn't run fast enough had to retest every few days until they met the required time.

Many freshmen prepare for their first season by lifting weights to increase their size. Often they put too much emphasis on becoming as big as possible. But it takes more than sheer bulk to play college football. Although size and strength are important, it's a mistake to ignore the importance of speed, agility and endurance. Football at Nebraska has evolved toward speed and explosiveness. It doesn't take long for our new players to understand this, but it's not easy to get our point across to them before they join our program.

For the past two years we have been limited by an NCAA rule that allows only 105 players in fall camp. We normally carry about 140 to 150 on our squad, so 40-odd players couldn't be invited to our initial practices at fall camp. The rest of our squad starts practice on the first day of classes. Fortunately, our classes usually start between August 20 and 25, so these players miss no more than the first 10 days to two weeks of practice.

I don't like the early limits on squad numbers because it often makes those not invited to the early practices feel as though they are second-class football players. Those who report later are an important part of our team. It's always difficult to decide who should come back early and who should be invited late.

These early limits on players are ridiculous when you examine how it affects a Division I football program. We save about $3,000 on room and board by not having the extra 30 to 40 at fall camp. While the rule does save a few thousand dollars, it doesn't make much sense when you realize that major football programs generate millions of dollars.

Our fall football practice begins with three days of freshman orientation. The freshmen are allowed to practice on two of the three days. Each evening they receive material from our academic counselors about the library, classroom sites, strategies for taking notes, and other information to help them adjust to the University of Nebraska.

The varsity players were tested on August 8, and each of the 83 varsity players passed the 300-yard shuttle run and set records for team speed and explosiveness. Evidently, they hadn't slacked off on their training during the summer—they were ready to play.

Our first day of varsity practice, August 9, was a difficult one. Monte Christo, our fourth-string quarterback, suffered a torn anterior cruciate knee ligament in a noncontact drill. As he planted his foot to make a cut, he was hit on the shoulder. Apparently, the stress on his ligament was sufficient to tear it. During his first year with us, Monte had surgery on his back and thumb. It's not unusual for a player to undergo surgery to repair an injury. Unfortunately for Monte, he had so many and they occurred so early in his college career.

Monte's injury immediately put us in another dilemma at quarterback. We were planning to redshirt our two freshmen quarterbacks so we were down to two scholarship quarterbacks, Tommie Frazier and Brook Berringer. We also had Matt Turman, a walk-on with playing experience from the year before.

As it turned out, Monte's knee injury was the only major surgery we had during the entire season. But I was very uneasy when he hurt his knee in our first practice.

The humidity and temperatures were high. That wasn't unusual for Nebraska in August, but the overall heat index made it difficult for the players to practice. Fifteen players left our first afternoon practice with heat cramps and several of them had to be given intravenous fluids to stop the cramping.

We held our first scrimmage on August 13. Fortunately there were no serious injuries. Chris Norris, our third-string fullback, strained his knee, but the trainers thought it would only keep him out for a couple of weeks. The competition was intense during the scrimmage. As often happens, the defense played better than the offense during the first scrimmage of the year. It usually takes the offense a little more time to develop.

Several players were upset about the Riley Washington incident. There had been animosity between some young African-Americans in the community and those who played on our team. The hostility had been going on for several years and was often triggered by several local youths who were envious of our football players. Our players always receive more attention for being part of the football team than most of them either want or deserve. Since Nebraska doesn't have a professional team, our players and coaches receive more attention than those at most colleges. Sometimes our players don't handle their celebrity status like they should. I'm sure these local youths feel threatened by our athletes, and I'm also sure there are times when our players don't show much respect for others.

As the threat of animosity from the young men in the African-American community continued, I became more concerned. The shooting incident made things worse between our players and the local youths. I knew there was a possibility either side might strike back.

During a team meeting, I discussed how important it was for our players to remain calm. I read a verse from the Bible to make my point. "Love is patient, love is kind, it does not envy, it does not boast, it is not proud, it is not rude, it is not self-seeking, it is not easily angry, it keeps no record of wrongs" (1 Corinthians 13:4-5). Reading this verse may seem a bit strange coming from a football coach, but I really believe that much of the violence on the streets today can only be dealt with by forgiving one another. So often a young person feels honor bound to retaliate when offended by someone else. The incident may start with only an exchange of words, but it often escalates to guns or knives. A few meaningless insults between young people can easily lead to violence. At some point, someone has to break the cycle of violence and retaliation. Unfortunately, the idea of turning the other cheek is rarely practiced and hardly understood by many people in our society.

Our staff has tried to teach our players how to avoid conflict. We've taught them to either ignore insults or laugh at them. But sometimes they may have no choice but to meet force with force. We constantly counsel them to avoid parties and places that make drinking or drugs available. We also let them know the best way to steer clear of a difficult situation is to avoid it to begin with. It doesn't make sense to attend a party where you know someone will pick a fight with you. Riley did back away from a conflict with Cole. Unfortunately, Abdul Muhammad later fought Cole, which ultimately led to gunfire.

Sometimes these predicaments are similar to the old West gunfights. Someone would pick a fight with the gunfighter who had the best reputation in hopes of making a name for himself.

There have been incidents where someone has picked a fight with a football player to enhance his reputation. In fact, there have been times when the person who picked the fight had absolutely no chance to win it. However, I think they felt the fight would prove their toughness or courage.

The football player is put in a "no win" situation. If he backs down from the conflict, he loses face. If he goes ahead with the quarrel, he most likely will be seen as the aggressor because of his obvious size and strength advantage. I don't mean to imply that our football players are always blameless. However, I do believe much of the time our players are not looking to create problems.

We attempted to remove as many potential problems as we could by having all our players' guns used for hunting locked up at the campus police headquarters. These rifles and shotguns had to be checked out and checked in by the owners. Anyone possessing a handgun or a weapon not secured by campus police was subject to dismissal.

On August 17, we had a major scrimmage, our second of the season. The heat and humidity were unbearable. The temperature on the artificial surface must have been around 105 degrees. I was proud of how the players endured the conditions. They were really hurting toward the end of the scrimmage. I'm always concerned about an injury when the players become so exhausted. Fortunately, no one was hurt. We scrimmaged our top two units against each other and then practiced our punts and kickoffs at full speed. I was very pleased with the practice. Things went about as well as I could have expected.

We ended our fall camp on August 18. I was relieved when we finished camp with only a few injuries. Although the camp had been very demanding physically, our players kept a positive attitude. Everyone seemed focused on having a great team. When our players are fixed on the proper goals, we rarely notice any complaints. When our team isn't focused on the right things, then even trivial problems become big issues.

We had our autograph day on August 19. Normally, it would have been prior to the start of practice on August 8. However, we wanted to make sure that all of our players could be included. We were now able to invite the remainder of our squad to practice since the 105-player limit was no longer in effect with the start of classes.

Each year, several thousand fans show up for a two-hour autograph session. This year was no exception. I really dislike signing autographs and I've reached a point where I would never ask anyone for an autograph. It seems like a strange custom. It's hard for me to understand why people will wait in long lines for a signature. I imagine most of the autographs are eventually forgotten in the garage or the attic. However, autographs seem to be very important to some people. I'm afraid our autograph day became self-defeating. Many people drove several hours, stood in line for a couple of hours and still didn't get an autograph. It seemed like everyone wanted to get Tommie Frazier's and Lawrence Phillips' autographs. I left the field after two solid hours of signing and there were still people wanting an autograph. Since we had scheduled a team meeting, there was simply no way to sign more.

Throughout fall camp there had been a great deal of speculation about who would be the starting quarterback. We let Brook Berringer and Tommie Frazier continue to compete for the starting spot. We carried their grades over from the spring scrimmages and combined those grades with fall scrimmage grades. Both quarterbacks benefited from the competition. They knew they couldn't afford to have a bad scrimmage or even a bad practice if they wanted to be the starter. Tommie knew his passing needed to improve, so he spent more time on his throwing. He became a better passer, just as Brook worked hard to improve his option ability, which was the weakest part of his game. Coaches love to go into the season with at least two proven quarterbacks. I knew it was uncomfortable for them to compete against each other every day, but it was the only fair way to choose the starting quarterback.

On August 22, I attended a Touchdown Club Dinner in Omaha with the other coaches on our staff. More than 800 people set an all-time attendance record for the club. Naturally, the enthusiasm was very high. Many of our fans wouldn't settle for anything less than a national championship. Anything else would be considered a bad year. As a coach, you know how difficult it is to win a national championship. Many variables are nearly impossible to control. Injuries, officiating, weather and strength of your schedule enter the national championship picture. I was apprehensive about the incredibly high level of expectation.

Our final scrimmage before the first game against Oklahoma State, was held on August 23. Our top two offensive and defensive teams ran 120 plays against each other. The hitting was intense. We finished the scrimmage feeling very fortunate to have only one minor injury. Joel Makovicka, our No. 3 fullback, sprained his ankle. To have come through the fall camp without losing anybody for the season to an injury, other than Monte Christo, was fortunate.

August 24, was an eventful day. We told the media that Tommie Frazier would start at quarterback ahead of Brook Berringer. The main difference was that Brook had three more turnovers than Tommie did in the spring and fall scrimmages. In our grading system, turnovers are costly. Their overall performance was close, except for the turnovers. They were both good players and we intended to play both in the first few games of the season. We planned to start Tommie and later play Brook a series or two early in the second quarter. During the second half we planned to play the quarterback who played the best in the first half. After the first four or five games, we intended to declare the starter whom we would stick with, unless he was injured.

Riley Washington practiced for the first time on August 24. I told the team before practice that Riley was cleared to join us since I hadn't seen any evidence that indicated to me that he shot Jermaine Cole. Riley had consistently maintained his innocence and his two former teammates corroborated his story. My biggest problem was that so many people thought he was guilty. I notified our team that Riley wouldn't play in a game until we had more conclusive evidence. I hoped the preliminary hearing, which was held on the same day we played Oklahoma State, would shed more light on the matter.

Our game with Oklahoma State had been moved from early October to August 31. We changed our schedule to accommodate ESPN for a night game. Just a few days before the game, we were told my father-in-law, Stan Tederman, had passed away quite suddenly in his hometown of Holdrege, Nebraska. My wife, Nancy, and I got the word around 10 p.m. Several hours later we arrived in Holdrege. My mother-in-law, Mary, who is in her 80s, held up as well as could be expected.

My father, Charles Osborne, had passed away in February of 1984, only a few weeks after we had lost the national championship to Miami 31-30. I've always regretted not visiting him after the season was over. Instead, I had plunged right into recruiting and did some speaking engagements. His life had a great impact on mine, so I knew what Nancy was feeling.

My mother passed away just prior to the 1994 Orange Bowl game we lost to Florida State 18-16. She had suffered a stroke 12 years before, and I had watched her battle a very difficult and deteriorating physical condition through those 12 long years. She always showed great courage and maintained a positive attitude throughout her last years. With Stan's death, we were both running out of parents. It made us more aware of the passage of time. It seems when you begin to lose those you've known and loved the longest, you begin to think about the things that are really important.

Stan managed a department store for many years in Holdrege and practiced his hobby of carpentry until just a year or two before his death. Stan did much of the carpentry around our house and our cabin at Lake McConaughy. He left something tangible for us to remember him by. His funeral was held Wednesday, August 30. I flew to Holdrege to attend the funeral and immediately returned to Lincoln so I could catch the team plane.

We had a short workout under the lights the night before the Oklahoma State game. Following our workout, we held a brief meeting followed by the players' usual snack. It seems college football players eat every few minutes. They'll eat between 3,500-6,500 calories a day. Fortunately, they work hard enough to keep their body fat surprisingly low.

I was encouraged by the attendance at our chapel service the next morning. Several players surprised me by showing up. We don't require attendance at chapel services, so I'm never sure who will attend. Even though chapel services are strictly voluntary, I encourage our team to consider the importance of spiritual values. During my coaching career, I've found that players who have a strong spiritual dimension often set the tone for a football team. They follow a moral compass that points them in the right direction. Also, a spiritual commitment usually leads to an unselfish attitude, which is a necessity for any team.

Gary Lower, a regional director for the Fellowship of Christian Athletes and a former track coach at Oklahoma, led the chapel service. Gary has an easy manner and is very effective in expressing his faith to athletes and coaches. We also had Mass for our Catholic players which was also well attended. With chapel and Mass combined, more than half of our players attend a worship service before most games.

After the worship services, we held a brief meeting that was followed by a long wait for the game to begin. Night games are always particularly difficult. We've never found a way to make the time pass quickly before a game.

I'm always especially uneasy before the first game of the season. There is really no way to be sure how good your team is until you play your first game. Even spring ball and fall practices are not always true indicators of how good a team will be. When you are practicing against yourself, everything is relative. You may have a great offense and a great defense, yet look really ordinary because they are so evenly matched. On the other hand, you may look spectacular either offensively or defensively because the competition is poor.

Oklahoma State had an experienced football team and a new coaching staff. Bob Simmons, the defensive coordinator at Colorado the year before, was now the head coach for OSU. With a new staff at Oklahoma State, we weren't sure how to prepare for them. We thought their defense would resemble what Simmons ran at Colorado, so we looked at a lot of Colorado tape. We were totally in the dark when it came to their offense. Their offensive coordinator was also new and we had practically no idea what he might do.

Once we got underway, however, it was clear we didn't have much else to worry about. We moved the ball almost at will—accumulating 671 yards of offense. Our offensive line showed they were ready to replace the four outstanding linemen we lost. Tommie played well, connecting on a 76-yard touchdown pass to Reggie Baul. Brook played a series in the second quarter and played a good deal in the second half. Our main area of concern was with our backup defensive players. They allowed Oklahoma State to break a few big plays and score 21 points.

As we returned to the field to start the second half, a strange thing happened. Apparently, the players were so engrossed in their thoughts that only a few of them heard me say that it was time to leave the locker room. Not looking behind me, I led a small group of players down to the field. Then, much to my surprise, I discovered most of the football team was still in the dressing room. As our small group ran on to the field, we were only a couple of minutes away from the kickoff. I had to send a manager back to the locker room to get the rest of the team. We really had to scramble to line up for the kickoff—not a good way to start the half.

It was a warm 99-degree night in Stillwater, yet our players didn't tire. Lawrence Phillips rushed for 153 yards, including a spectacular 80-yard run where he dodged several defenders. Terrell Farley, a junior college transfer, made an interception which he returned 29 yards for a touchdown. It was our first defensive touchdown in two years. Kris Brown, a true freshman, did a nice job as a place-kicker, and Jesse Kosch also looked good as our punter, though we only needed to punt once.

The final score was 64-21. We were ahead 50-7 when we began to substitute for our first-unit players during the middle of the third quarter. It looked like we could have a very good team.

Probably, the most gratifying part of the game was the play of our inexperienced players. Sixteen players started their first Nebraska football game. They all played like veterans. Sometimes players tighten up in their first major college game, but I saw no evidence of it in Stillwater. We had played well on national television, and we suffered no major injuries. I was pleased with the start of the season.

7

AGENTS
AND THE NCAA

Because of an NCAA investigation, we were unsure if Lawrence Phillips would be allowed to play in the Oklahoma State game. The NCAA had quizzed Lawrence about his contact with sports agents. Jesse Martinez, who worked for a sports agent named Steve Feldman, named Lawrence as one of several athletes whom he claimed had violated NCAA rules. Evidently, Martinez spent several years working for Feldman from his office in Newport Beach, California. Martinez was a "recruiter" for Feldman. A recruiter is the initial contact person for an agent. He moves into a community to network with any athlete the agent wants to sign. The typical recruiter will offer cash, cars, clothes or other enticements to influence the athlete. Of course, these incentives violate NCAA rules. Whenever a recruiter negotiates a contract before the student-athlete finishes his eligibility, the athlete makes himself ineligible.

Jesse Martinez had a falling out with Steve Feldman, and he

blew the whistle on Feldman and several athletes whom he tried to recruit. I was surprised when Lawrence Phillips appeared on his list. Apparently, Lawrence had been contacted by Jack Verner, another recruiter for Feldman. In November of 1994, Verner took Lawrence, a junior, and three of our senior athletes to lunch. NCAA rules were violated when Verner drove them to the restaurant and then paid for their meals. The incident was never reported until Martinez told the NCAA. During the summer of 1995 the NCAA investigated Lawrence Phillips' activities with Feldman and Verner.

Lawrence said he only accepted the luncheon from Verner. However, Martinez claimed Feldman paid for a flight from Lincoln to California. Martinez also said Feldman paid for a meal when we played Miami in the 1994 Orange Bowl.

Al Papik, our Senior Associate Athletic Director and Compliance Coordinator, investigated the claims made by Jesse Martinez. He got receipts from the restaurant in Lincoln and from Tina McElhannon. Tina was the Executive Director of the group home where Lawrence lived from the age of 13 until he came to the University of Nebraska. Receipts showed that Tina McElhannon paid for the flight Lawrence took to California. He also found that Lawrence didn't eat with Jack Verner at Bennigan's restaurant in North Miami Beach. Al had each credit card transaction examined dated December 29, 1994, when the supposed dinner in Miami took place. Neither Steve Feldman's nor Jack Verner's name appeared on any of the credit card transactions for that day. Lawrence insisted all along that he didn't dine with Jack Verner in Miami. Several other players said that Verner was in Miami at the time and offered to take them to dinner, but no one accepted his offer.

After Al Papik sent his report to the NCAA, Lawrence was cleared to play against Oklahoma State. However, once Lawrence was cleared of any wrongdoing with agents, the NCAA decided to investigate Lawrence's relationship with Tina McElhannon. They wanted to know if any rules were violated by her providing financial assistance to Lawrence. Tina leased a car for Lawrence, gave him spending money and paid for his travel between Lincoln and California. We always assumed this aid was legitimate and complied with NCAA rules since she acted as his legal guardian. The NCAA wondered if she was his legal guardian and whether she was providing permissible aid.

Eventually, Al Papik traveled to California to document Lawrence's relationship with the Tina Mac Group Home. He found that she acted as the legal guardian for Lawrence Phillips, so her financial aid didn't violate NCAA rules. Unfortunately, the NCAA ruling wasn't made until much later in the season, so we didn't know if Lawrence would be allowed to play until nearly game time against Michigan State. For the first two games of the season Lawrence was in limbo concerning his playing status until shortly before each game.

It's amazing how many hoops you have to jump through to please the NCAA once you've been accused of wrongdoing. Much of the material Jesse Martinez gave the NCAA concerning Lawrence was inaccurate. He even called a local newspaper with his charges. The paper then investigated Lawrence's relationship with the group home and even dug into his personal history. Lawrence is a private person, so he was upset by the unwelcome interest in his personal life. Lawrence reimbursed Steve Feldman $20 for the lunch in Lincoln, probably much more than it cost. Finally, the NCAA dropped their investigation of Lawrence.

I don't believe Lawrence thought he was wrong by going to lunch with Jack Verner. I do wish he had been more careful. We do our best to encourage our players to check with the coaches or Al Papik before they do anything questionable. To Lawrence's credit, he probably had many chances to take cash or other inducements from agents, yet neither the NCAA nor anyone else uncovered any evidence that Lawrence profited from agents. And it certainly wasn't due to lack of effort that nothing was found. Lawrence was scrutinized by both the NCAA and the University of Nebraska. I'm sure if he had done anything seriously wrong, somebody would have uncovered it during the investigations.

Riley Washington's preliminary hearing was held on August 31, the same day we played Oklahoma State. They held the hearing to decide probable cause in the shooting of Jermaine Cole. If they found probable cause, then Riley would be bound over for trial.

Willis Brown was called as a witness. He testified that he did not believe Riley shot Cole. A key witness for the prosecution, Bernard Stewart, was also called. Stewart had been a witness in a federal case and was thought to be a reliable witness by the prosecution. Bernard was with Cole the night of the shooting and was present when he was shot. I assume the prosecutor felt Bernard would identify Riley as the shooter. Instead, he was unable to identify Riley as the person who shot Cole. When Bernard left the courtroom, he told an investigator that Riley's body type didn't match the person who shot Cole. I'm sure this was a blow to the prosecution since Bernard was a key witness.

Cole was also called to testify as a witness in the trial. In order to testify he had to be released from jail, where he was awaiting trial for assaulting his girlfriend. Originally the defense wasn't sure Cole would even appear in court. However, he didn't have much choice since he was in jail. Cole claimed Riley shot him, which was all that was needed to bind Riley's case over for trial. Prior to the preliminary hearing, Cole had told acquaintances that he didn't know who shot him.

Riley was bound over for trial on September 8. His attorneys from the Public Defender's office told me to expect his trial to occur no earlier than the spring of 1996. It was interesting that Cole testified that Riley shot him and then tried to shoot him again at close range, yet told others he didn't know who shot him. He also was not accurate in describing the clothing Riley wore even though he said Riley was only a few feet from him.

There is a curious parallel to Riley's case. Brendan Holbein, one of our wide receivers, was shot by a .38-caliber pistol when he was an innocent bystander at a party in September of 1994. The bullet grazed his side, so he received several stitches. There was a possibility he might not play that week against UCLA. The media showed interest in the story because his injury could affect his ability to play but showed little interest in who shot him. During the next 14 months, I was never asked about the shooting incident by the media. No one seemed to be interested if the person who shot Brendan had been identified or charged with attempted murder.

Although Brendan's shooting occurred on September 10, 1994, the preliminary hearing was not held until the spring of 1995. Eric Alford, one of our football players, identified a young man from Omaha as the person who shot Brendan. However, the defendant failed to appear at the preliminary hearing and the judge set a new date. At the second hearing, the judge listened to the evidence and bound the case over for trial. He set the trial date for July of 1995. Unfortunately, Eric Alford tried out for the New England Patriots during July. Because Eric left Lincoln, the judge dismissed the trial and the pretrial proceedings had to start over.

A third preliminary hearing was scheduled on November 16, 1995, 14 months after the shooting took place. A different judge was assigned to the new preliminary hearing. This judge dismissed the case stating "the state failed to meet its burden of proof," though the case had previously been bound over for trial. Because the third scheduled preliminary hearing occurred 14 months after the shooting and was heard by a new judge, it appeared much of the evidence may have been lost in the process. Reference was made to Eric Alford's inconsistent statements about where he was standing at the time of the shooting. Understandably, Brendan and his family were upset at the way the whole episode played out.

It was interesting that the case was delayed several months just because the accused failed to show up at a preliminary hearing. This, in turn, delayed the trial to a time when Eric Alford, the key witness, could not be present. Had Brendan's case been given the scrutiny that Riley Washington's received, I wonder if the case would have fallen through the cracks. The fact that there was so little interest in who shot Brendan seemed to contrast starkly with the interest in cases where a football player was the accused.

On September 5, I notified the *Daily Nebraskan* editors that I would no longer grant individual interviews to their reporters. I was upset by their cartoon that showed Riley Washington in prison garb shackled to a ball and chain. The cartoon implied that

Riley Washington was guilty as charged. They also published a cartoon of Lawrence Phillips in a car with money flying out the windows. The newspaper was insinuating that one of our players was guilty of accepting illegal extra benefits. The *Daily Nebraskan* is a student newspaper, so I felt it was unfair for them to treat fellow students in this way. I was disappointed that students would be less sensitive to our players' problems than other media outlets. Local newspapers didn't run cartoons that were inappropriate, but the *Daily Nebraskan* did. I didn't try to influence other coaches or players to follow my ban. It was my personal decision.

The only way I could carry out this interview policy was to visit with writers individually after practice. The *Daily Nebraskan* was included in all scheduled press conferences, but I wouldn't let them personally interview me. As a result, I spent extra time each evening talking individually to members of the media who came to practice.

Most schools don't meet with the press after each practice. Many of them hold a press conference only once or twice a week. However, at Nebraska it has become a tradition to meet with the press daily. It does get a bit tiring after I've already put in a long day, especially since I still have much to do at night.

Generally, I enjoy the members of the local press. I see them so often I can't help but appreciate what they do. It's not easy to write a column on football every day. I'm sure some reporters are as tired of covering football as I am having to talk about it.

Naturally, the *Daily Nebraskan* staff was not happy about my decision. I felt badly for their sports reporters, who did a good job. I hated to make their jobs more difficult, but I couldn't seem to get my point across to their editorial staff any other way. In past years, I tried to reason with them with little success, so I felt I needed to do something drastic. I also wanted my players to know I was willing to support them if I thought they were treated unfairly.

We had nine days to prepare for Michigan State after playing our opener on August 31. Michigan State presented another interesting challenge. For the second straight game our opponent had a new head coach. Again, our coaching staff was not entirely sure how to prepare against Michigan State's new coach, Nick Saban. He had been the defensive coordinator for the Cleveland Browns where he did an outstanding job. As a result, we looked at lots of Cleveland Brown videotape when we prepared to play them. As was the case against Oklahoma State, we were in the dark on what Michigan State might run offensively.

We had an enthusiastic week of practices as we prepared for Michigan State. Former Nebraska football coach and athletic director, Bob Devaney, spoke to our team before the game in East Lansing. Bob began his college coaching career as an assistant to Duffy Daugherty at Michigan State after coaching high school football in Michigan. He appeared sentimental and somewhat emotional as he talked to the players. I was pretty emotional as well. Bob means a lot to me and it was good to see him back where he began his career. Once more he was part of the game he loved.

Our team took the field and played well, although we weren't as sharp or intense as we had been against Oklahoma State. We had 666 yards of total offense with more than 500 of those yards on the ground. Tommie Frazier was hurt early in the game when he suffered a bruised thigh and couldn't finish the game. Brook

Berringer replaced Tommie and played quite well. We were very fortunate to have a second quarterback who could have started at most other schools. His experience, ability and poise made him an outstanding quarterback.

Reggie Baul made a tremendous catch on a 51-yard pass from Brook, and Lawrence had a great day rushing for 206 yards on 22 carries. He made several spectacular runs including his fourth touchdown run of the game. The ball was snapped directly to him when we were in the shotgun formation. He broke the play up the middle, cut to the left sideline and sprinted into the end zone.

Our defense allowed Michigan State to score only 10 points. I was impressed with our defense because their senior quarterback, Tony Banks, was a big athlete with a pro arm. Nick Saban seemed upset with his defense after the game. I hoped their performance had more to do with our offensive play than poor defense on their part. It felt good to leave East Lansing with a 50-10 win. I was more confident about our team, and I began to think this might be the best team I had coached.

When we arrived in Lincoln, I noticed Lawrence was still in his seat sleeping. Most of the players had already left the plane when I noticed him. As I began to gather my belongings, I had an impulse to spend a few moments talking with him. I even thought about asking him over to my home that evening. Lawrence often seemed lonely, and at that moment, he seemed vulnerable and a little sad even though he had played an excellent game. I know he probably would have thought it was odd for me to invite him over to my house, so I simply congratulated him on playing a good game. I also reminded him to get treatment for his sprained ankle in the morning. He thanked me for my compliment and agreed to see the trainers the next day.

Turner Gill called me the next morning at 5:30. He told me Lawrence had attacked a girl and the police had called Turner and asked him to come to the scene of the assault. When I hung up the phone, I knew nothing would be quite the same again for Lawrence, the football team, or myself for the rest of the season.

8

A DIFFICULT WEEK

When Turner Gill called me about Lawrence Phillips' arrest, it began one of the most difficult and strangest periods of my coaching career. Lawrence was a central figure in this episode. It's hard to understand someone's behavior unless you know his background.

Lawrence was born in Little Rock, Arkansas, the oldest of two boys. His father left the family when Lawrence was an infant, and when he was three, Lawrence, his mother and brother moved to Los Angeles. The first few years of Lawrence's life in California were stable. He and his mother had a good relationship and he did well in school. In fifth grade he attended several different schools, but even so, he did well and was a good student.

When Lawrence was 12 years old, a male friend of his mother's moved in with their family. He didn't like the man because he ordered Lawrence around. Lawrence told me he couldn't tolerate someone who "gets in his face." According to people at the youth home, where he lived from age 13 until he enrolled at Nebraska, he felt his mother chose to live with the friend rather than him.

Consequently, Lawrence left home at age 12 and stayed with a friend for a short time before he was picked up by the police for truancy. He was placed in a foster home, then in a community residence and finally in a group home. Tina McElhannon ran the group home that went by the name "Tina Mac's."

Things went well for Lawrence at Tina Mac's. He liked the staff and was in a structured environment that agreed with him. While in the group home he graduated from junior high and enrolled at West Covina High School. Before his junior year, he left West Covina because he wanted to join a better football team and attend college preparatory classes.

Lawrence transferred to Baldwin Park High School and his football team won the city championship during his junior year. Lawrence took a great deal of pride in that accomplishment.

According to people at the group home, Lawrence didn't use drugs or alcohol. They also said he never had any serious problems with the law. He was highly recruited by many colleges during his senior year. He finally narrowed his choices to the University of Southern California and the University of Nebraska.

NCAA rules permit the head coach to make only one recruiting visit, so I saw Lawrence only once in Los Angeles. George Darlington, the assistant coach who recruited him, myself, Lawrence and one of his high school administrators, Ty Pagone, met in Mr. Pagone's home. Lawrence seemed reserved and didn't talk much. I thought he was a bit shy and cautious. He listened intently to what I had to say as if he were trying to evaluate whether I could be trusted.

We had a good recruiting visit with Lawrence. It appeared that many people at Baldwin Park believed Nebraska would be the best school for him to attend. They seemed to think it would be good for him to get away from Southern California.

Lawrence had to complete quite a bit of school work during his senior year to meet NCAA standards. A few schools even quit recruiting him because they weren't sure he would be able to meet the requirements. Although he had much catching up to do, he did complete his work and qualified for a scholarship. This effort showed that Lawrence was goal-oriented and was capable of doing well in school.

When Lawrence arrived in Lincoln, Nebraska, he was surprised to find few minorities in our community and had to adjust to an environment that was very different from his group home. Lawrence was with our team for only a short time when he got into a fight with another freshman player. I learned that Lawrence was the aggressor in the fight, so I suspended him from his first game at Nebraska.

There were days when Lawrence appeared lonely. Although he knew many players on the team, it didn't seem like he had many close friends. I always felt he was a little sad and withdrawn. Playing football was the only thing that seemed to make him completely free of whatever was troubling him.

As a student, Lawrence was a sociology major and wanted to manage a group home like Tina Mac's. Soon after beginning college he began to date the young woman he would later have problems with. Out of respect to her and her family, I will not refer to her by name but rather will refer to her as the "victim." Lawrence became attached to her, and since he had few close friends, their relationship was very important to him.

Lawrence had some success in his freshman year. He played most of the game when we beat UCLA 14-13. In that game he carried the ball 28 times for 137 yards. Although he was inexperienced, it was obvious he was a tremendous competitor who had great potential.

Later that season he played an important role in the Orange Bowl game we narrowly lost. He replaced an injured Calvin Jones and ran for 64 yards on 13 carries in the second half.

Lawrence's mother re-entered his life when he came to Nebraska. She worked in Lincoln for a while and then moved to Omaha during his sophomore season. He received a call from his brother in December of 1993, while we were preparing for our national championship game against Florida State. His brother lived in Omaha with his mother and told Lawrence she was being abused by a boyfriend. Once Lawrence heard this from his brother he disappeared for two days. Lawrence had played outstanding football all year and he had a chance to play for the national championship, so we were surprised when he missed practice.

After two days Lawrence returned to practice. Apparently, he had resolved whatever problem his mother had. However, because his absence was unexplained and unexcused, his participation in the Orange Bowl was in jeopardy. Lawrence was very protective of his mother and obviously put her welfare ahead of his football career.

The team captains asked that Lawrence be allowed to play because many of them didn't want to risk losing the championship without his help. Lawrence had a very good reason for missing practice, yet he didn't ask permission to be excused. We would have given him permission to miss practice if he had simply asked. I told the captains we would suspend him for the first half of the bowl game and then let him play in the second half if needed. Of course, Lawrence played in the second half and played well; however, we still lost the game.

With Lawrence's talent and a great offensive line, he had an excellent chance to win the Heisman Trophy in 1995. He was the leading returning vote-getter for the Heisman Trophy from 1994. Now he was bigger and faster, so everyone expected great things from him.

Nearly two weeks before the Michigan State game, an acquaintance of the victim and the acquaintance's father met with me to discuss Lawrence's troubled relationship with the victim. Later I called the young woman and told her I had heard that she was having trouble with Lawrence. She admitted there were problems with their relationship. She told me she was frightened and described an incident in which Lawrence had acted in a threatening manner toward her.

I told her I was going to visit with Lawrence, but I promised her I would not mention our conversation to him, as she requested. I promised her I would tell him to leave her alone, or risk being suspended from the football team. I gave her my home and office phone numbers and I asked her to call me if he tried to contact her. I then warned Lawrence to steer clear of her or risk suspension. He knew there would be consequences if he didn't follow my instructions.

A few days later, Scott Frost told me the victim occasionally visited him and said she was frightened of Lawrence. Scott was a transfer to the University of Nebraska from Stanford. I explained to Scott that Lawrence had been advised to stay away from her. I asked Scott to stay out of the situation. I felt his involvement could only lead to further problems. In talking with Scott, I got the impression that he and the victim were casual acquaintances. However, I discovered later that Scott and the victim occasionally dated each other. I didn't think that the relationship was serious, but they were more than acquaintances.

Not only did I prohibit Lawrence from seeing the victim, I also had him receive counseling from Jack Stark. Jack is our sports psychologist, and I felt he could help Lawrence overcome some of his problems and help him stay away from the victim. Jack and Lawrence met twice a week and discussed how he could develop more positive relationships. Although I wasn't sure the counseling would solve all of Lawrence's problems, I didn't know what else could be done at that point.

As it turned out, nobody took my advice. Lawrence and the victim had communication both on the phone and in person. I believe the victim wanted to break off their relationship; however, often people who are in a bad relationship aren't sure how to emotionally distance themselves from the other person. From Lawrence's standpoint, he seemed to believe that there was still a relationship of sorts. He still cared for her and wanted to believe that she felt the same way.

The victim gave Lawrence a ride just before we left to play Michigan State. Lawrence also called her the night before the game from East Lansing. Based on their phone conversation, he thought they might meet following our return from Michigan. Instead he spent the evening with a former teammate, Ed Stewart. Later that night he returned to his apartment.

Around 3:00 a.m. he got a phone call from someone who

knew the victim. According to Lawrence, this "friend" asked him to come to an apartment complex where he was shown the victim's car. At first, Lawrence wasn't concerned about where her car was parked because he thought she was visiting a female friend. Then the "friend" pointed at a mailbox with Scott Frost's name on it and told Lawrence the victim was with him. Lawrence became very angry. He rang Scott's doorbell, but no one answered. The victim was sitting on the floor watching TV while Scott was asleep. Both were fully clothed.

When Lawrence rang the doorbell, the victim looked out the window and saw Ed Stewart's car in the parking lot. She guessed Lawrence had borrowed Ed's car since she knew that his was in the repair shop. Immediately, she woke Scott. Since no one answered the doorbell, Lawrence climbed the outside of the building and entered the apartment through a balcony door. Scott tried to shut the door, but Lawrence got inside before Scott could close it. The victim ran into the bathroom thinking Lawrence might be breaking into the apartment.

Eventually, Lawrence forced his way into the bathroom and confronted the victim. He remembered saying, "Why did you lie to me?" Lawrence then dragged her down three flights of stairs. He grabbed her by the hair and at times by her shirt. When Lawrence and the victim reached the bottom of the stairs, Scott tried to separate Lawrence from the victim.

A young man who was visiting the apartments, Matthew Roland, tried to help Scott wrestle her away from Lawrence. According to Roland, when Lawrence pulled the victim away from them, she hit her head on the wall. At some point, the back of her head was cut. Lawrence became somewhat distracted and

Scott and Matthew helped her reach the safety of a neighbor's apartment. At that point, Lawrence beat on the mailboxes with his hands and cut them quite badly. He also kicked the security door before leaving the building.

Several apartment residents heard the disturbance and called the police. Once the police arrived, they notified Turner Gill. When he arrived around 5:30 a.m., the officers reported some of the details of the assault to him. I was asleep when Turner called me with the news of Lawrence's assault. He informed me that the victim was taken to the hospital to be treated for a cut on the back of her head. He thought the victim would be all right, but she was pretty shaken by the attack. The victim did receive several stitches on the back of her head. She received bruises and scrapes from being dragged down the stairs. Her shirt was torn and bloody, so she left it with a person who lived in the apartment complex. Although she was treated and released from the hospital in a short time, she was understandably traumatized by the event.

Some reporters said the victim's head was beaten against the mailboxes when they showed the damaged boxes on TV. Actually, Lawrence's fists had crushed the mailboxes in his anger.

No one heard from Lawrence through most of the following day, Sunday, September 10. I was worried he might try to harm himself since he probably thought he had blown his chance to play football at Nebraska. Both football and his relationship with the victim were very important to him, so I believed he might turn his anger inward and hurt himself.

Later that day, about 12 hours after the assault, Tina McElhannon called me from her home in California. Lawrence was on the line also. I figured he was afraid to contact our coaches so he called Tina. She pled Lawrence's case and asked me to give him another chance. Lawrence felt terrible about what happened and was ready to accept any punishment we handed out. I told him I needed to find out more about what had happened before I could decide his future as a player. I asked him to see me right away. I guessed he was somewhere near Lincoln, but he did not tell me where he was.

I advised Lawrence to contact an attorney and turn himself in immediately. Later that night after he turned himself in, he was released on bond. I was very upset at him because I assumed he disregarded my warning and had stalked the victim. I was sure his playing career at Nebraska was over.

I met with Lawrence the next day and suspended him from the team. There would be no practices, meetings, or games—no association at all. I did tell him I would not make his suspension final until I could examine the details of the assault.

As I visited with him, Lawrence broke down and cried. I must admit, I had a few tears in my eyes as well. Lawrence had built an emotional wall around himself that was very hard to penetrate. I had never seen the person behind the wall until that moment. Lawrence had lost most of the things he valued in life, and I could sense his anguish.

Later, in talking to Barbara Thomas, Tina McElhannon's sister, I mentioned that Lawrence shed some tears. She was very close to Lawrence since she worked at the group home. She was surprised when I told her about Lawrence's reaction. She had known him since he was 13 years old and had never seen him cry. Lawrence always maintained a tough exterior and refused to show any weakness or sensitivity.

Monday morning I got a call from Angela Beck, the University of Nebraska women's head basketball coach. She was the victim's coach and asked me to meet with the victim and her parents in her office. Many people thought that I had driven to the victim's home a considerable distance away in order to persuade her family not to press charges. This was totally inaccurate. The only meeting I had with them was in Angela's office and we never discussed whether or not they should press charges.

We met about noon on Monday, roughly 30 hours after the attack. I expressed my concern and sympathy to both the victim and her parents. We discussed the victim's safety. I also told them that I needed to find out more about what had happened before I made a final decision about Lawrence. There were things I was learning about the whole matter that were causing me to rethink my earlier impression of Lawrence's role. I was particularly interested in Lawrence's relationship with the victim, especially since they had continued to see each other. I also was interested in the person who brought Lawrence to the victim's apartment. This person obviously knew the victim's whereabouts and might be a friend or acquaintance of the victim.

I told the victim and her parents that I was not certain as to what I would do with Lawrence. I might even let him rejoin the team under certain circumstances. The victim's parents were understandably worried about their daughter's safety. I could relate to their fears since I'm the father of two daughters. A major concern was to protect their daughter from Lawrence. The athletic department provided her with 24-hour protection and counseling. My meeting with the victim and her parents was cordial. Later I talked to the parents on the phone two or three times about their daughter.

To make matters worse, Damon Benning was involved in an incident with a former girlfriend on September 9. The former girlfriend went over to his apartment and asked for several of her belongings. Apparently, Damon placed them outside the apartment complex door. She not only refused to take them, but she used a key to scratch his car. While she scratched his car, Damon only watched. Finally, she tried to enter his apartment. Damon was afraid she would damage his apartment, so he kept her out. Since she couldn't enter the apartment she called the police and charged him with assault.

I talked to Damon on Monday, September 11. He was adamant that he did nothing to his former girlfriend. He felt he had shown tremendous restraint by allowing her to damage his car and in resisting her attempt to enter his apartment. The press had a field day with both Lawrence and Damon being charged with assault. Damon told me two young women who lived in his apartment building witnessed the incident and were willing to discuss it with me. Once the women heard the inaccurate reports about the incident in the press, they offered to help Damon. When I talked with the young women, they corroborated Damon's story. One girl told me she was surprised by how well Damon restrained himself.

At the press conference on Tuesday, September 12, I told the press that I believed Damon was innocent of the assault charge based on what I knew. Since Lawrence Phillips had been suspended, I planned to play Damon in our next game against Arizona State. I felt badly for Damon and his parents because he received so much negative publicity from both the local and the national media. Some reports erroneously stated he was charged with sexual assault. It took nine days before the authorities dismissed the charges against Damon. Meanwhile, his reputation was severely damaged and the football team was embarrassed even more.

When a high-profile athlete is cleared of any wrongdoing, the follow-up story rarely receives the same attention as the initial story. Damon's story was no exception.

In the September 25 issue of *Sports Illustrated*, Gary Lacey, the Lancaster County Attorney, accused me of "using (my) influence to disrupt the criminal justice system." Apparently, Lacey was upset about my speaking to witnesses. In Damon Benning's case, Damon asked me to call the young women who witnessed the alleged assault. Authorities had the same opportunity to talk with the people in the apartment building. As it turned out, Damon was falsely accused.

When I talked to people who knew something about an alleged crime, they were almost invariably current or former players or their friends. I did not go out and conduct my own investigation as Lacey alleged. Whatever I tried to find out was to aid in knowing what to do about a player's playing status, not to "disrupt the criminal justice system."

The same *Sports Illustrated* article had Lacey accusing me and one of my assistant coaches, Kevin Steele, of withholding evidence. They reported that we retrieved and concealed a weapon used in a criminal investigation. The gun belonged to one of our players, Tyrone Williams.

Kevin called Ken Cauble, the Chief of the University of Nebraska Police, before he even got the gun from Tyrone and asked him what to do with it. Chief Cauble told Kevin to leave the gun locked in his desk until he picked it up. He promised Kevin he would pick up the gun and take it to the proper authorities.

Lacey knew full well that we had followed Chief Cauble's instructions to the letter. I had personally told Lacey exactly what we had done. I had met with Lacey, Lincoln Police Chief Tom Cassady, University of Nebraska Chancellor Graham Spanier, and Athletic Director Bill Byrne in the Chancellor's office to explain the entire gun scenario. I told them we secured the gun only two days before the National Letter of Intent signing day. Once the gun was safe in Coach Steele's desk and he notified the authorities, we began concentrating on recruiting. I assumed that Chief Cauble had picked the gun up and turned it over to authorities. Concealing a weapon was the last thing Coach Steele and I had on our minds. I was surprised that the local authorities weren't quite pleased that we had recovered the gun.

Shortly after Kevin Steele obtained the gun from Tyrone, I went to the police garage and looked at the car that had been allegedly shot at by Tyrone. I told the officer that showed me the car that a .22-caliber pistol was involved. Apparently, the officer went to his superiors and told them about my comments. I assumed the police had the gun. It would have been stupid to tell the officer about the gun if we were trying to conceal evidence.

I don't have a clue why Lacey told *Sports Illustrated* we deliberately withheld evidence. Now there were some reporters in the national press as well as the Lancaster County Attorney making serious accusations.

I feel our criminal justice system is generally quite good; however, it usually takes months or even years for some cases to be settled. Since we play a football game every week, it's hard for me to wait on the justice system before I decide on a player's status.

I believe it's important for a player's view to be told. I know this annoys law enforcement authorities, but often only the person who makes accusations gets his or her views expressed in the police report and the press. The accuser's perspective is not always accurate. Therefore, even though the police do the best that they can to get all the facts, police reports often don't represent all that actually happened. Since police reports are available to the press, contents of police reports are often all that the public hears about an alleged crime.

Although a person who is accused of a crime in our country is presumed to be innocent until proven guilty, the public often equates an accusation with guilt. If the person accused of the crime had at least two or three days before the charges became public, many misunderstandings could be avoided. Sometimes taking a little time to gather information and then putting the whole matter in perspective would help a great deal. Often new facts clear the suspect of any crimes.

Once charges are filed and then publicized, you can't put the genie back in the bottle. Authorities are often reluctant to dismiss or to reduce charges for fear that the public might think they are soft on crime. An athlete or any well-known person accused of a crime immediately attracts so much publicity that it becomes very difficult to conduct an accurate, unimpeded investigation of the facts.

There was a larger than usual press gathering at the weekly press conference before the Arizona State game. Many national news outlets attended because of our recent problems with Lawrence Phillips, Damon Benning and Riley Washington. We were portrayed as a football program that was out-of-control.

One writer labeled us "another Miami." At the press conference, I denied that we were another Miami. It was a mistake for me to publicly respond to the writer's comparison. My response simply gave the press another reason to condemn us.

Later I wrote Butch Davis, the football coach at Miami, and Dr. Foote, the President of the University of Miami, and apologized to them. I was trying to defend our program, but my comment was taken by some as a criticism of Miami's program. I meant Miami's past problems were not the same problems we had. I regret some people thought I was trying to make Nebraska look good at the expense of Miami.

A columnist later criticized us for recruiting Lawrence Phillips. He suggested that we failed to notice Lawrence's character flaws when we recruited him. George Darlington, the assistant coach who recruited Lawrence and I disagreed with the column. We look at character, and we screen our players as carefully as possible before we offer them a scholarship. If there is evidence of drug problems or problems with the law, we stop recruiting them. We also won't recruit an athlete whom we don't believe can do well enough academically to graduate.

When we recruited Lawrence, the NCAA rules allowed our coaches three recruiting contacts in his home community. As the head coach, I was allowed to make only one of those visits. It's difficult to know a recruit very well by spending only a few hours with him. Of course, we do write and call each athlete we recruit, but still it's not quite like a personal visit. We did check Lawrence's background as much as we could. As far as we could detect, Lawrence had no arrest record. He was recommended by the administrators in his group home and the people at Baldwin Park

High School. He displayed sufficient intellect and a good work ethic when he met NCAA academic requirements to qualify for a scholarship during his last two semesters of school.

It's true that Lawrence didn't have much parental support and he wasn't always raised in the best environment possible. However, these reasons were not enough by themselves to eliminate him as a recruit. If we only recruited those players with ideal family backgrounds, we wouldn't have too many players to recruit. And I don't think it's fair to penalize an athlete because he didn't have as much family support as other athletes.

Since I began coaching at the University of Nebraska as a graduate assistant coach in 1962, I have noticed some definite shifts in our culture. These shifts have made coaching more difficult and complex. At the same time, these cultural shifts have given a coach an opportunity to make real differences in the lives of young people. The following represent five major areas where I have seen a great change.

First, the stability and solidarity of our families have deteriorated a great deal over the past 34 years. Approximately 30 percent of the babies born in our country each year are born outside marriage and hundreds of thousands of others are aborted.

A high percentage of our teenagers live in single or no-parent homes. When I first began recruiting, it was rare to find a recruit who was from a single parent family—now it's common.

I don't mean to say that young people from single parent families are not receiving adequate parenting, many are. However, there is no doubt that children growing up in single-parent homes, on the average, live in more financially and emotionally impoverished circumstances. Generally, they don't do as well academically and have more personal problems.

I'm amazed at the number of young people who are growing up without either parent. Each year we have several players on our team who have no family support. Some of these players defy all odds by raising themselves and making it on their own. But family instability often results in troubled and insecure young people.

Second, the environment is more hostile and dangerous for young people. We have the highest homicide rate for young people of any nation in the world. During the past nine years, eight of our football players or recruits have been shot. I can't recall a single shooting incident involving our players in my first 25 years of coaching.

Michael Becton was a walk-on player from New York City who left after a semester because of financial problems. Not long after he returned home, he was fatally shot while dribbling a basketball down the street. Leon Otis was another walk-on player for a brief time. After leaving due to financial and personal problems, he was fatally shot in Los Angeles. Broderick Thomas, who was a linebacker for us, went on to play for the Tampa Bay Buccaneers where he was shot in the arm at a Tampa parking lot. Kenny Wilhite was shot in St. Louis before he attended Nebraska. He still has the bullet lodged in his arm. Abdul Muhammad was shot in Los Angeles during his summer vacation by someone who was driving by his apartment. Willie Harper, Jr. was shot in Omaha before he ever enrolled at Nebraska and almost died of the wound. Brendan Holbein, one of our current players, was grazed by a .38-caliber bullet in the random shooting discussed earlier. Chris Norris, a former fullback, was shot in the arm with a .22-caliber bullet in 1993.

Chris was shot by a young man named Michael Berkland.

Berkland was found guilty on November 22, 1993. He was originally charged with second-degree assault and eventually pled guilty to a reduced misdemeanor charge. He was also charged with carrying a concealed weapon. Berkland was sentenced to two years probation. As far as I know, there was no publicity about this shooting. It seems his two-year probation for shooting Chris Norris was very lenient. Had Chris Norris or Brendan Holbein done the shooting, there would have been a good deal of publicity. I wonder if Brendan would have walked away with no penalty as his alleged assailant did. I wonder if Chris would have been given probation as the person who shot him was. I do not buy the theory that athletes are treated better than others by our legal system because of their status as athletes.

The University of Nebraska is located in the Midwest city of Lincoln, Nebraska. Most people would think Lincoln is a safe place, and compared to most cities of this size it is very safe. Yet both Brendan and Chris were shot in Lincoln.

Michael Becton's mother wrote me a letter not long after he was killed in New York City. She wrote, "We are taking one day at a time, some days one moment at a time. It feels like a bad dream that we will awake from and see our beautiful son and brother with that ever-present, big smile on his face." Her letter represents the anguish many parents feel whose children have been victims of violent crimes.

Our country not only leads the world in teen homicide, but our teen suicide rate is also first. To have a young person die by his or her own hand has to be one of the most terrible tragedies a family can endure. The loss is usually compounded by endless questions about what the family might have done differently to avert the tragedy. I have dealt with families after a suicide, and it is truly a devastating experience.

Third, drug and alcohol abuse is another common problem that impacts our players and society. Most crimes of violence involve drugs or alcohol. Hard drugs such as cocaine and heroin continue to be a problem. Marijuana use is on the increase again after being on the decline for many years. By far the biggest problem we see at the University of Nebraska is alcohol. Many high school and college coaches tell me this is the greatest drug problem for their athletes as well.

Alcohol abuse is particularly dangerous because so many adults fail to realize how many young people have a problem with it. I believe many adults underestimate alcohol because they are so familiar with it. A few adults even think it's a good way to keep young people from taking hard drugs. Alcohol won't keep their young people "safe." Alcoholism is just as destructive and just as fatal as other types of addiction and often is the precursor to other drugs. Alcohol abuse represents the major part of the drug problem in our country for young people.

Fourth, television, movies and music add to the problems young people face today. It's not hard to see the changes in the entertainment industry during the past 30 years. Young people are continually exposed to violence and sexual promiscuity, and they are influenced by what they hear and watch. There is a persistent theme in much entertainment that promiscuity is attractive and that it does not have serious consequences. I believe that there is a clear link between the violence and promiscuity seen and heard in the media and the violence, unwanted pregnancies and sexually transmitted diseases in our society.

Fifth, values have shifted a good deal during the past 30 years. A poll released by the Princeton Research Center in Princeton, New Jersey, in April of 1992, showed that 69 percent of Americans think there are no moral absolutes concerning right or wrong. In other words, what is right or wrong depends on the situation. This means that about 7 out of 10 adults maintain that theft, adultery, or even taking someone's life is not absolutely right or wrong and might be justified in certain situations.

Stephen Covey, in his book *The Seven Habits of Highly Effective People,* pointed out that in reviewing 200 years of literature dealing with success, he noticed that literature written in the first 150 years of our country's existence defined success in terms of what he called a character ethic. Foundations of success had to do with such things as "integrity, humility, fidelity, temperance, courage, justice, patience, industry, simplicity, modesty and the golden rule." In other words, success was defined by these positive character traits.

Covey noted that in the past 50 years there has been a shift from a character ethic to what he calls a personality ethic. The personality ethic is focused more on public image, positive mental attitude or even methods of deception. In other words, the shift was from issues of character to issues of personality and appearance.

Because of the erosion of moral absolutes and a superficial definition of success, many young people have nothing solid to hold on to. They don't have a moral compass to point them in the right direction.

Most people recognize many of these negative forces that make it more difficult to parent, teach and coach young people.

Our players are no different from other young people in society. It's impossible to insulate them from problems found throughout our culture.

Teachers and coaches have had to carry more and more of the responsibility for young people that parents normally have had to bear. Many of our best teachers, the ones who care the most, burn out early in their careers as they struggle to help young people who are hurting so much. We ask more and more of these people and yet don't pay them as well as we do so many occupations that require less training and are less stressful.

As Bobby Bowden says, "The problem with being a coach is that you must be a teacher, a father, a mother, a psychologist, a counselor, a disciplinarian and Lord-knows-what-else . . . When you have 100-plus young men, boys who come from all kinds of environments, you are going to have problems." Amen.

Although we had difficulties, our team practiced well for Arizona State. I was apprehensive as the game approached. I was afraid that our players and coaches might be distracted by our problems. I've seen other teams that have fallen apart after they began losing their focus on playing football.

The theme on our media guide was *Staying Focused*. Now, more than ever, we needed to stay focused on football, not our problems. With Lawrence Phillips suspended and Damon Benning sidelined with a pulled hamstring, we were getting seriously short of I-backs. We started Clinton Childs at I-back against Arizona State and planned to rely on a true freshman, Ahman Green, to back him up. Arizona State played well enough to win against Washington in their opening ballgame, but barely lost to them. They won their second game handily and appeared to be a very good team.

I didn't really know what to expect when we took the field. Clinton Childs quickly put my mind at ease by running our opening play 65 yards for a touchdown. Eventually, we put together one of the most memorable first halves of offense in my coaching career. We scored 63 points and had 508 yards of total offense at the half. Clinton Childs rushed for 143 yards and two touchdowns before leaving the game when he was struck on the knee by a helmet. Ahman Green ran for 111 yards and two touchdowns. Tommie Frazier ran for two touchdowns and completed 7 of 10 passes for 191 yards. We ended the game with 686 total yards. Our offensive line was exceptional.

Arizona State was especially aggressive in trying to stop the run, so we threw some deep play-action passes. Clinton Childs even threw a pass to Clester Johnson for 34 yards.

The defense did a good job at times, but gave up too many big plays. We gave up 461 yards to Arizona State. However, many of those yards did come against our second-unit players.

On the last play of the game, our offense did something I would later regret. With about 45 seconds left in the game, we had the ball. It was third and 12, so I called a hook pattern to Lance Brown. When Lance arrived at the hook point, the safety played him tight, so Lance went deep. Once Lance went deep, Matt Turman threw a perfect pass to him for a 39-yard touchdown. I didn't want to run up the score, but when the defensive back overplayed Lance on the pass pattern, Lance made the adjustment and the touchdown resulted. The Nebraska players who were in game when we scored were third- or fourth-string players.

The Arizona State coach, Bruce Snyder, was very angry with me after the game. He even talked about the play on national television. I tried to explain what happened. I don't know if he understood or even wanted to understand what I said. I sent him a letter of apology, but didn't receive a response from him. It was the only offensive touchdown that we scored in the second half. We scored one other time on an interception by Terrell Farley.

Despite all this, I couldn't have been prouder of the way our team played. There was no question that everyone in our organization, players, coaches, and everyone else associated with the program understood that we were in a tight spot. They all pulled together for an outstanding performance. The best response that we could possibly make to all of the criticism was on the field. Many of the attacks we had endured were difficult to answer in any other way.

9

HITTING BOTTOM

On Tuesday, September 19, Lawrence Phillips entered a plea of no contest to two misdemeanor charges. One count was for trespassing, the second count was for assault. I was not sure what sentence he would receive for the two misdemeanor charges, but I didn't think it would involve a jail sentence. Once the court set Lawrence free, I knew there would be a problem with Lawrence and his victim attending the same school.

Lawrence issued a public apology on the same day that he pled no contest to the misdemeanor charges. I believe he was genuinely sorry for the assault and for the turmoil that resulted.

Lawrence was banned from the athletic training table because the victim was a member of the women's basketball team. He was given a food allowance so he could eat on his own. For the most part, he ate fast food. He also had to stay away from the weight room and training room whenever the female athletes were lifting weights or being treated by trainers.

The ban on the training room was unfortunate for Lawrence because he had to go without treatment for the ankle he sprained when we played Michigan State. He didn't complain about the ankle, so several weeks passed before I knew he hadn't received treatment for it. Lawrence was also required to attend class regularly and was expected to make satisfactory academic progress.

The most pressing issue, as far as I was concerned, was to have Lawrence receive a complete medical evaluation to find out his mental and emotional condition. A local psychiatrist, Dr. Boman Bastani, and Jack Stark, our team psychologist, recommended we send him to the Menninger Clinic in Topeka, Kansas. The Menninger Clinic has an outstanding reputation as a psychiatric clinic, and we felt it was perhaps the best clinic in the country for him to receive a complete psychological profile. After his Menninger evaluation was over, Lawrence would still need to comply with university disciplinary policies and with the legal requirements of the courts.

I couldn't make the decision to send Lawrence to the clinic by myself. He too needed to decide if the clinic evaluation was necessary. He was already receiving calls from agents who were willing to sign him. Many of them were offering him money if he would sign with them before the NFL draft in the spring. For Lawrence, it would have been much easier to take the advance money and wait for the draft. Instead he would choose the more difficult path.

Lawrence visited with me about his decision. He knew it wouldn't be easy to face his problems, but he was willing to take responsibility for what he did. He really didn't want to go to the Menninger Clinic because he is a private person. His past is painful, so he rarely discusses it. He knew the Menninger Clinic experience would involve a thorough examination of his past. I'm sure this was a major concern for him.

Because of Lawrence's strong desire to finish the football season, he chose to follow the steps I outlined for him. He knew he had no chance of finishing the season if he violated any of my requirements, which were to attend class regularly, attend counseling three times a week, have no contact with the victim, and comply with the requirements of the court and the university.

Lawrence drove to the Menninger Clinic with an assistant strength coach, Kevin Coleman, on September 19, where he spent the next four days undergoing an extensive evaluation.

We had bad news on September 19. I received a report that Clinton Childs had sustained a more serious knee injury than we first thought. Dr. Pat Clare, our team orthopedic surgeon, reported that Clinton suffered a crack in the bone near his knee. Normally, an injury like this would keep a player sidelined for about six weeks. This meant Clinton could miss the rest of the season. With Lawrence Phillips suspended indefinitely and Damon Benning bothered by a pulled hamstring, we were getting really thin at I-back.

Fortunately, Ahman Green and James Sims were still healthy. Although he was a true freshman, Ahman was starting to play well and James Sims, a walk-on, was doing well in reserve. I was glad we started the season very deep at I-back.

Pacific was a team that really should not have been on our schedule. Pacific was a replacement for Utah State who withdrew from their contract with us on short notice. I felt bad for Chuck Shelton, the Pacific coach, because he was having to play a tough schedule that included Arizona, Oregon and Nebraska. Pacific was forced to play teams like Nebraska because they were desperate to keep their football program alive financially. Pacific was making more money playing an away game against a team like Nebraska, than they were from a home game in Stockton, California. While there may not be much risk of losing a game against a team like Pacific, most fans are disappointed if the score isn't lopsided. However, if you do run up the score, you often embarrass the other team and are usually ridiculed by the media for trouncing them.

Coach Shelton is an excellent coach who has struggled at several schools that aren't known for their football programs. While he was head coach at Drake, his teams pulled some amazing upsets. Drake eventually dropped football and Chuck got a job at Utah State. He stayed at Utah State for several years, but their football program lacked the resources needed to beat many top teams. Eventually, he took the head coaching job at Pacific. Every time we played one of Chuck's teams, we always felt that they were well prepared, played very hard and did about as well as they possibly could against us. Pacific also dropped their football program at the end of the 1995 season. I know it was an unfortunate surprise for Chuck and his players.

There were no surprises in the Pacific game. We scored 21 points in the first quarter. Our coaches began substituting freely during the second quarter, so in the second half we only scored 14 points. The final score was 49-7.

Although Damon Benning was slowed by an injured hamstring, he played well. With the injury to Clinton Childs and the suspension of Lawrence Phillips, we were fortunate to have a player like Damon replace them. He rushed for 173 yards and three touchdowns on only 10 carries. Unfortunately, he sprained his ankle in the third quarter and had to leave the game.

James Sims, our fifth-string I-back, managed to score a touchdown, but he was also injured and was forced to leave the game with a sore back. As a result, by the time that the Pacific game was over, only Ahman Green was completely healthy. Ahman had rushed for more than 100 yards against Arizona State and now he did the same against Pacific. He was gaining confidence with each carry and was beginning to look like a big-time back. We didn't play inspired football, but considering the fact that we were so heavily favored, our play was respectable. I thought that the University of Pacific players gave a tremendous effort. I know Chuck had to be proud of how they played, though the final score was one-sided.

Our defense also played well. We held Pacific under 200 yards and the one score they had came against some of our reserve players. It looked like our team was improving on both sides of the football.

We rushed for 569 yards and threw for 162 more; however, we only completed 16 of 36 passes. The completion percentage was not what it should have been. The 36 passes we attempted were the most attempts we had made at Nebraska in 22 years. We weren't throwing so much to score points, but instead we were trying to improve our passing game. Most of the throws were short to medium range passes, so there was no attempt to run up the score.

Riley Washington made his first appearance of the year in the Pacific game. Although he had practiced, we held him out of the first three games until everyone had time to evaluate the evidence against him.

It was tough for me to keep my mouth shut about the evidence in Riley's case. I was privy to some facts that I thought showed he was innocent. Yet, many who didn't have access to all of the facts seemed to feel he was guilty of shooting Jermaine Cole. Most of the publicity about Riley's case came from his accusers. And much of it did not seem to be accurate.

I met with Joan Leitzel, the Acting Chancellor at the University of Nebraska; Jim O'Hanlon, our Faculty Representative; Jim Griesen, Vice Chancellor for Student Affairs; Ken Cauble, the University of Nebraska Chief of Police; Riley Washington; Bill Byrne, our Athletic Director; and three people from the Public Defender's office who presented some of the information they had gathered on Riley's case. After reviewing the evidence that was available to us, it appeared that most in the room felt like I did, that Riley didn't shoot Cole. There was some uneasiness about the possibility of Riley being reinstated to play football. We all knew the national press would make an issue out of his return and would not have many facts concerning the case.

The attorneys advised me that Riley's case would probably not come to trial until well after the first of the year. If I waited for the court's verdict to reinstate Riley on the team, he would have missed the entire season. This did not seem fair to Riley, especially since I believed him to be innocent. I knew my decision would not be popular or even understood since most of the public had not seen as much of the evidence as I had.

Before we played Pacific, I read an article that recounted a similar choice Coach Shelton had to make. While head coach at

Utah State, two of his players were accused of rape. He, too, was convinced of his players' innocence. They were later found innocent, but he went ahead and played them before they were found not guilty. I'm sure Chuck caught some flack over his decision. But I doubt he received the national media scrutiny that we had at Nebraska.

When Riley was finally allowed to play against Pacific, he caught two passes and played a fair amount of the game. It's often hard for me to judge the mood of a crowd during a game because I wear headphones. But I didn't think there was much of a negative reaction from the crowd when Riley entered the game. It seemed that Nebraska fans and the local press were at least willing to take a wait-and-see attitude on Riley. However, we all knew that the national press would probably not be so forgiving as the fans and local press.

The day after the Pacific game, when I arrived at work, our linebacker coach Craig Bohl told me another player might be charged with a crime. Craig thought the player would be charged with rape later that day. I was in utter disbelief that after constantly preaching at our players to steer clear of trouble, that one of them may have done something terribly wrong. The player who was accused of rape denied the allegation, but by now I had heard so many denials that I wasn't sure who to believe.

The player claimed that he met a girl, whom he had known for about a year, at a party after the Pacific game. He noticed that she had consumed a lot of alcohol while at the party. Eventually, they spent some time outside the house before returning to the party. According to witnesses, the young woman appeared in a good mood when she returned to the party. She continued to drink to the point where she had to be helped to a car so she could be taken home.

Apparently, she awoke about 5:00 in the morning and began crying. She told her roommates that she had been raped the night before. They immediately took her to the hospital and had her examined. She later blamed the player for raping her earlier in the night. I had definitely reached the end of my rope. If the accusation was true, I felt very bad for the young woman. I also felt bad for the whole team as the difficulties they had encountered to date were nothing compared to what might now happen.

I told the player to get an attorney as soon as possible. I did not try to find out anything else about the case except what I heard during his brief explanation. I wanted to make sure no one could accuse me of tampering with the criminal justice system. The player had absolutely no idea which attorney to select. Just as Riley Washington picked his attorney at random from the yellow pages, now this player would do likewise.

10

WHERE
FAITH COMES IN

The three-day stretch following the Pacific game was a personal low point for the season. We were undefeated and obviously had a great football team. But I felt as if we had lost every game. The recent rape allegation against one of our players was the proverbial straw that broke the camel's back. This recent incident had literally and figuratively brought me to my knees.

My faith is very important to me regardless of our success on the field. Now it seemed as though my faith had become even more crucial. I think that what a person believes about God will affect how he sees himself, the world and other people.

Victor Frankl, a Jewish doctor who survived several years in various concentration camps during World War II, wrote, "I am absolutely convinced that the gas chambers of Auschwitz, Treblinka, and Maidanek were ultimately prepared not in some ministry or other in Berlin, but at the desks and lecture halls of nihilistic scientists and philosophers."

Frankl meant that the Holocaust was a result of faulty thinking by the elite in Nazi, Germany. Much of this thinking was influenced by the philosopher, Frederick Nietzsche. Nietzsche believed that religious people, and particularly Christians, stood in the way of man's journey to become Superman. He theorized that there was no God, and man was the measure of all things. His philosophical viewpoint influenced Adolph Hitler and later Benito Mussolini. The philosophy of Nietzsche, as carried out by Hitler, unleashed one of the most depraved movements in the history of mankind.

Today, I believe we are again fighting this battle between theistic and anti-theistic ideology. If you believe there is a God who loves you and gives your life direction, you will behave differently from someone who doesn't believe there is a God. The atheist, someone who doesn't believe in God, views man as the measure of all things. If this is the case, then self-interest tends to dominate behavior. I've seen a definite shift toward a narcissistic, what's-in-it-for-me attitude in recent years. Since our nation has become more anti-theistic, it has started to reflect a society that is more self-absorbed.

Ravi Zacharias, in his book *Can Man Live Without God,* said: "And in our search for morality and happiness outside of God, we have effectively lost all three—God, morality, and happiness."

I see many students and faculty today who openly scoff at anyone who believes in God. Faith is more than an intellectual exercise, however. Zacharias has an interesting passage in his book:

"The well-known social critic Dennis Prager, debating the Oxford atheistic philosopher Jonathan Glover, raised this thorny question: 'If you, Professor Glover, were stranded at the midnight hour in a desolate Los Angeles street and if, as you stepped out of your car with fear and trembling, you were suddenly to hear the weight of pounding footsteps behind you, and you saw 10 burly young men who had just stepped out of a dwelling coming toward you, would it or would it not make a difference to you to know that they were coming from a Bible study?' "

I have heard the pounding footsteps enough to know the truth of what he says. Often how someone faces his death has everything to do with how he lives his life—either with expectation, a clenched fist or a whimper.

Sometimes people say, "It doesn't matter what you believe since all religions are really the same." As I have studied the religions of the world, it seems that nearly all, except Christianity, ignore the idea of grace. And grace is what I am greatly in need of. I have come to the understanding that I fall so far short of godly perfection that it's only by grace that I can possibly be approved in God's eyes.

As I have gotten older, the concept of grace has affected me more and more. As a younger man, I unwisely tended to think that I could achieve a great many things through my own efforts—even God's approval. The longer I've lived, the more I realize that I have been able to earn very little that has lasting value through my own efforts.

Tom Landry, the former coach of the Dallas Cowboys, apparently arrived in his belief system at the same place I have. In his autobiography Tom stated: "The most important lesson I've learned in my life is that God is so gracious that He accepts me, my failures, my personality quirks, my shortcomings and all. It's hard for a perfectionist like me, but I have to admit I can never be good enough. No matter how sound my strategy, how much I study, how hard I work—I'll always be a failure when it comes to being perfect. Yet God loves me anyway."

Jimmy Williams is an example of how important God's grace is. Jimmy came to Nebraska as a walk-on player from Washington, D.C. Eventually, he earned a scholarship and later became an All-American defensive end. The more honors he received, the further he seemed to withdraw from me and the other coaches on our staff. During his last months at Nebraska he even got to the point of not speaking with several coaches, including me. It was never clear to me what I did to damage our relationship, but it was obviously seriously damaged. I felt bad about the relationship, as I had always respected him as a player and a person.

Although I hadn't seen Jimmy for several years, I followed his successful career in the NFL. Later, I attended a summer camp of the Minnesota Vikings and, by chance, ran into Jimmy before their practice. Immediately, Jimmy threw his arms around me and gave me a big hug. I was amazed by his response to seeing me. As we visited, it was as if we were old friends. The entire incident was remarkable.

I found out later that Jimmy had experienced a spiritual conversion. He experienced God's love and grace in a new way in his life. I think his spiritual U-turn allowed him to reach out to people in a new way. He was no longer withdrawn. Even while he played professional football, he began a ministry to prison inmates. I've watched many players over the years commit their lives to God. Each time a player has turned away from his own devices and put his life in God's hands, I've witnessed a change in attitude and behavior. It's only by God's grace that any of us can truly love ourselves or others.

As I think about the dilemma many young people find themselves in today, I believe it is only through God's love and grace that many of them will experience forgiveness and meaning in life. Some experts who work with young people depend strictly on a conditioned model of behavior to understand and help them. This model claims that each person is a product of his or her experience alone. For example, if they have only known abuse and rejection, then it follows that they are only capable of relating to others with hatred, anger and isolation. However, I have seen players who come from very difficult backgrounds overcome their circumstances. Billy Graham explains it this way, "The strength for our conquering and our victory is drawn continually from Christ . . . The Christian now has resources to live above and beyond the world." God allows us to transcend our experience. Even though we have been abused, battered and rejected, we can still rise above our past and care about others and ourselves with God's help.

The author of the well-known hymn *Amazing Grace* was a former slave trader who no doubt did some horrendous things to his fellow human beings. Yet even he at some point felt that through God's grace he could be forgiven. For me, the life of Jesus represents the ultimate expression of grace in the world. God has extended His hand through His Son so that we might understand that we are accepted and forgiven just as we are.

I realize many don't share this belief with me. But it's important for me to write about my faith because it affects the way I act. Having experienced grace in my life, I hope to be a little less judgmental, a little more forgiving, and a whole lot more appreciative of the fact that someone like me could be considered worthy of God's love.

I hope that my conduct honors God as I deal with players, coaches, my family, and with how I use the resources that I have been given. I realize I fall far short of honoring Him at times, but I also realize this is why I need God's grace.

As I sat in a meeting following the report of the alleged rape, I felt as if I couldn't handle another problem. Finally, I simply surrendered the entire predicament to God. As I prayed, I experienced a sense of peace about the rape charge and the other problems. I wasn't sure of the outcome, but I knew our situation was in God's hands and He would use it for His purposes.

Not long after I was praying about the alleged rape charge, our player was cleared. Fortunately, the County Attorney's office had not pressed charges until the matter was thoroughly investigated. The player volunteered to take a blood test, and no charges were filed. I'm sure if the matter had been publicized before the player was cleared, there would have been another round of negative press that would have reached monumental proportions.

According to the campus police, the young woman who claimed to have been raped had also been causing one of our other players a good deal of grief. She concocted a fictitious romance with the player even to the point of buying herself an engagement ring and sending out wedding announcements. The player was puzzled but not overly alarmed. We all hoped the young woman would get some help before somebody suffered some serious consequences from her erratic behavior.

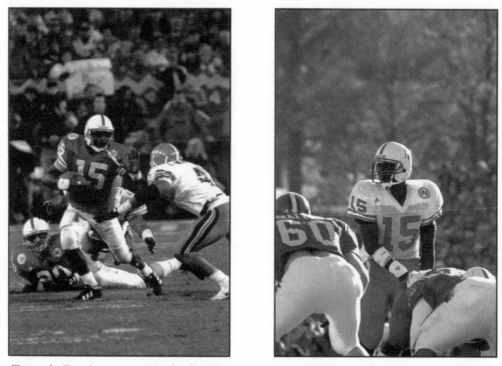

Tommie Frazier was not only the MVP for three straight bowl games, but he was definitely the key to our back-to-back national titles.

A sea of red surrounds Jon Vedral as he tries to grab a pass against an Arizona State defender.

Many of our players regularly join together for a postgame prayer.

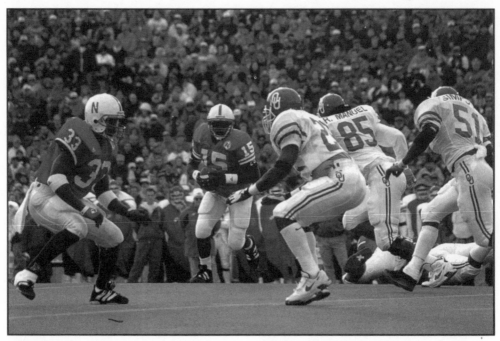

Many critics thought we should scrap our option attack for more of a pro-style offense. However, we proved with our back-to-back titles that it was still effective.

Farley blocks a punt against Missouri.

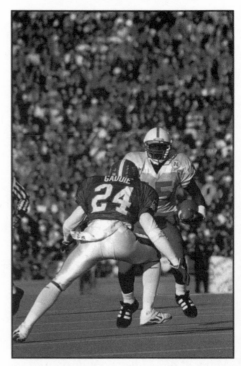

Frazier puts a move on Kansas defender.

Terrell Farley pulls down Florida's Danny Wuerffel. It's been said that defense wins national titles. Few would argue that point following our win in the Fiesta Bowl.

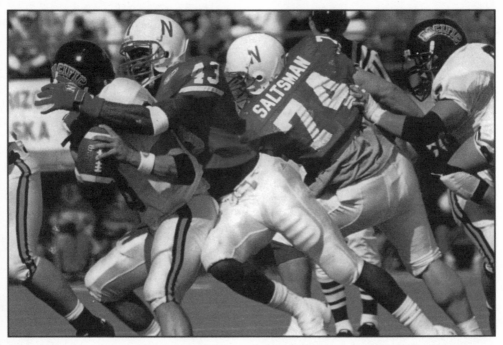

Terrell Farley was a pleasant surprise on defense. He was the Big Eight Newcomer of the Year as he developed into one of our best pass rushers.

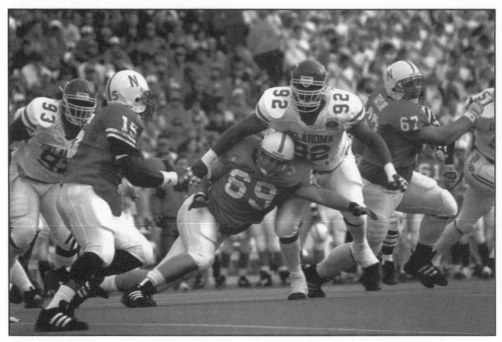

Steve Ott (69) leads the way for Tommie Frazier on this option. Steve was one of the offensive linemen who helped fill the four vacant spots on the line from '94.

Senior linebacker Phil Ellis was one reason our defense gave up few yards.

Tony Veland returns this fumble for a touchdown.

Freshman I-back Ahman Green developed into an outstanding running back during the '95 season. He has tremendous speed and agility.

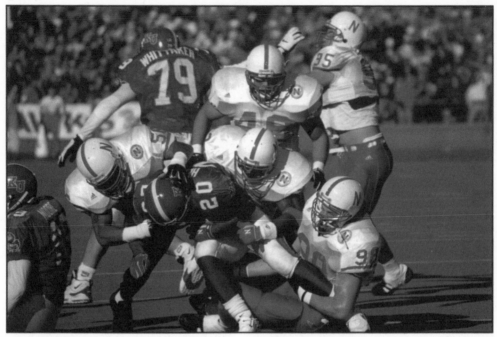

Our entire defense swarmed the Kansas offense in the second half. Most teams found it nearly impossible to run against our defense in 1995.

Grant Wistrom (98) and Jared Tomich (93) were two of the best rush ends we've had at Nebraska.

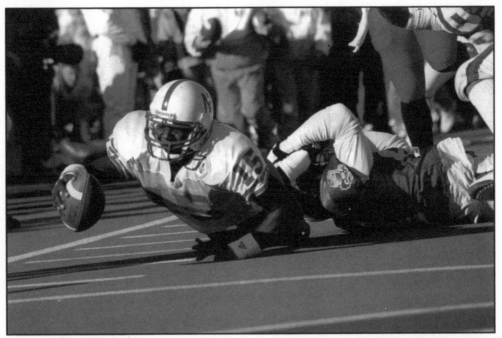

Tommie Frazier's talent to run and pass the football kept most defenses off-balance. Frazier's leadership ability added another factor that led to our success.

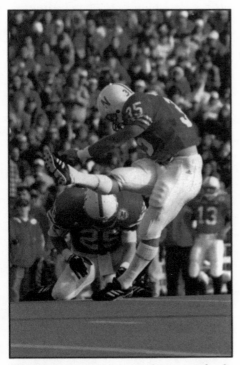

Kris Brown (35) stepped in as a freshman and helped us maintain a strong kicking game.

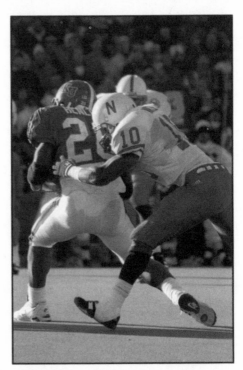

Mike Minter (10) was one of many quick and hard-hitting defensive backs in our secondary.

When Lawrence Phillips returned after being suspended for his off-the-field problems, he was out of shape. However, he was ready to play in the bowl game.

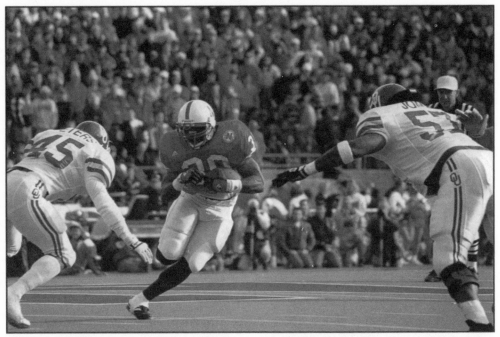

The combination of speed and strength has become a common trait for Nebraska I-backs during the past 20 years.

Fred Pollack leads Damon Benning around the end.

Because of injuries, I was thankful we had so much depth at I-back with players like James Sims.

Tommie Frazier's 75-yard run against Florida was amazing. The determination he showed on this run seemed to reflect the character of our team during '95.

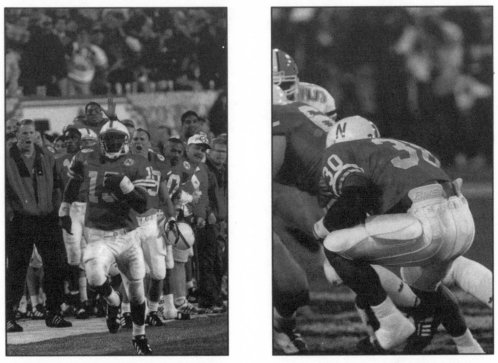

Our offensive explosion against Florida surprised everyone. Even Christian Peter tried to get into the act when he tried to return a fumble recovery for a touchdown.

*The 1995 team was perhaps the most unified team I've coached at Nebraska.
Negative publicity drew us closer together rather than pulling us apart.*

*We haven't won back-to-back national titles since 1970-71. Although our national
titles were a long time coming—many fans felt they were worth the wait.*

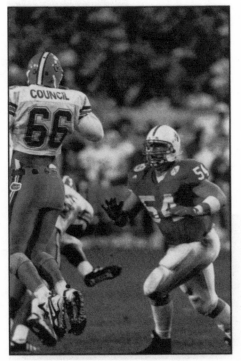

Besides being an Academic All-American, co-captain Aaron Graham was a leader on and off the field.

Clinton Childs not only ran the ball effectively for us from his I-back position, but he also returned kickoffs.

Brook Berringer (1973-1996)

As I went through the season, it became easier for me to take one day at a time. By not worrying too much about all of our problems, I could stay focused on coaching football. Although I doubt that God wants one team to win more than another, I do believe that He cares about every situation and will ultimately use every circumstance for good for those who love Him. To me, it's comforting to know that God either allows or causes all things to happen.

Our staff meetings are scheduled each day at 7:00 a.m. during the season. We begin our meetings with a brief devotional time. We have several coaches who take turns reading either a verse of scripture or some inspirational literature for a few moments. Generally, we discuss how the scripture or inspirational reading applies to each of our lives. Then we close our devotional period with silent prayer. The entire devotion usually only takes about five minutes, but it is our way of acknowledging our desire to serve God. I believe that if you yield your life to God, and seek to know Him better, then He will give you a proper perspective on life.

Often if we know a player is suffering emotionally or physically, we'll spend time praying for him as well. I believe there is power in prayer and it does make a difference in our lives. I spend time praying the morning of every game. During this time I pray for each player on our football team who will be playing. I pray for their safety and that they might make the most of their God-given talents. We also pray for our opponents at our chapel service. They are an important part of the game, and we hope that the actions of players on both sides will honor Him.

My experience has led me to believe that there are definitely some "fruits of the spirit" that accrue to those who practice a steady spiritual discipline.

First, I believe that spiritual discipline provides strength to serve. A little over a year ago, I went to Haiti with Don McClanen, who founded the Fellowship of Christian Athletes more than 40 years ago. Don took me to one of Mother Theresa's hospitals in Port-au-Prince where I talked with a Sister of Mercy who worked in the hospital. Though we only visited for a brief time, it was still the most meaningful part of the entire trip. She explained how she went through nine years of apprenticeship before taking her final vows to become a full-fledged Sister of Mercy. During this time she worked in a hospital for the dying. The patients were almost all under the age of two and very few ever recovered from their illnesses. Many children were infected with AIDS, and some were addicted to drugs because of their mothers' addictions.

The Sister worked many hours, seven days a week with few breaks. She was only able to visit her family once every 10 years. I asked her how she could endure losing so many children with her grueling work schedule. She explained that each sister was allowed one hour each day for devotions. It was that hour spent in prayer and meditation that gave her the strength to serve under such stressful conditions.

Though not nearly as virtuous, I could identify with the Sister's experience. I try to spend time each day in prayer or meditation. I also spend time in the scriptures each day. My time spent in this fashion has been a real source of strength to me. In the book of Isaiah it says that "those who wait upon the Lord will renew their strength. They will mount up with wings like eagles. They will run and not grow weary, they will walk and not faint."

I know that God provides the necessary strength to those who desire to serve Him.

Second, my faith has given me a sense of purpose, meaning and mission. Frankl, in his book *Man's Search for Meaning*, described how prisoners of Nazi concentration camps could survive the experience. He noticed those prisoners who had a sense of purpose and meaning had a better chance of survival than those prisoners who had lost hope. From his experience, he theorized that a sense of meaning and purpose in a person's life was almost as essential to well being as food, air and water.

With God removed from the equation, I have found life to be devoid of real meaning. You simply can't win enough games to satisfy yourself or others. No matter what your profession is there are always some accomplishments that exceed your grasp. When we try to measure ourselves by the expectations of others, we are bound to experience disappointment and disillusion. One of my favorite passages of scripture is found in the book of Hebrews where the apostle Paul says, "Therefore, since we are surrounded by such a great crowd of witnesses, let us throw off everything that hinders and the sin that so easily entangles and run with perseverance the race set before us, keeping our eyes fixed on Jesus, the author and perfecter of our faith, who, for the joy set before Him endured the cross, ignoring its shame, and sat down at the right hand of the throne of God." This verse of scripture illustrates almost all of the elements of running the Christian race successfully. Paul talks about simplifying our lives, getting rid of everything that drags us down and causes us to miss the mark and to run the race with perseverance. As the race is run, one's eyes need to be fixed on the goal—that of becoming more like Jesus.

As I have attempted to do this, admittedly with many failures, I have found meaning and purpose in my life that otherwise was missing.

Third, stability has been a another factor that has been an outcome of my spiritual journey. The coaching profession is very unstable. If you win enough games, you are often perceived as better than you really are. If you lose enough, you are sometimes treated as though you are inferior and incompetent. Usually, the truth lies somewhere in the middle. However, the world of athletics has very few places in the middle. You are often perceived as either the best or the worst.

The book of John starts out, "In the beginning was the Word, and the Word was with God, and the Word was God." I believe John's point is that Jesus always was, is, and always will be and He will not change. Once we realize that God is in control of our destiny, I believe we are better equipped to handle life's setbacks. The above three spiritual benefits have been very important to me, particularly during this past season.

We lost seven straight bowl games and went through 22 years of football without a national championship. Many people in the media and some fans would continually bring up this fact. I was often asked about how I felt about not winning the national title. My answer was always the same, "I believe I can leave coaching without winning the national championship or even another bowl game and still be satisfied with what I've done as a coach." I'm sure a few people thought I wasn't being entirely honest when I would repeatedly respond with this statement. But this was truly how I felt.

I've always enjoyed the relationships with the players and

coaches more than the trappings of success. So many coaches and players think they'll be satisfied if they win enough games or championships. However, the real secret of enjoying sports is to focus more on the process than the scoreboard. All I ask of my players or coaches is their best effort. Nothing more and nothing less. Sure it hurts to lose games—especially when you're very close to winning a key game or national title. But I don't obtain fulfillment solely from winning. I've always thought if we did the right things, the right way, often enough, then winning would take care of itself.

Monday, following the game with Pacific, we had a team meeting and I informed the players about the alleged rape, but didn't mention the player's name. I thought the press might report the story at any time, so I felt the players should be aware of the accusation. I guessed the players sensed that I was bothered by all the negativism surrounding our team. Apparently, they wondered how much more I could take.

Christian Peter and Phil Ellis both came in individually and visited with me the next day. Both were team captains and both expressed concern about the general situation and concern about how I was holding up. I thought I was doing well under the circumstances, but they felt the pressure was wearing me down. I found out later they were concerned that I might be thinking about resigning. I assured them I would be fine. I explained to them that none of us had any choice but to pull together and play hard.

Later the players called a team meeting without coaches present. While I'm not sure of everything that took place at the meeting, I do know the players voted to abstain from alcohol for the rest of the season. They also pledged to avoid parties or other questionable gatherings. No doubt they knew any incident, no matter how small, would be seen as national news. As far as I know, the team did an excellent job of following through on their vote. I'm not naive enough to believe that every player abstained from drinking or partying for the entire season, but there were no further reports of either.

Once the player was cleared of the rape allegation, everyone on the team was relieved. However, I did suspend the player for the upcoming game with Washington State. Since he was under the legal drinking age, I suspended him for using alcohol and for putting himself in a position that could reflect negatively on the whole team.

Even with all the negative distractions we still kept our focus on football. Our coaches knew our upcoming opponent, Washington State, would require a great effort on our part. They had been playing well and had a quick, aggressive, confident defense. They were also known for a sound passing game.

Although Washington State had been allowing less than 70 yards per game rushing, we ran for 428 yards against them. We also had 527 total yards of offense. However, I was bothered by the offense missing three scoring opportunities near the goal line. We didn't execute the way I had hoped in scoring situations.

Washington State had defeated UCLA the week before we played them and had momentum coming into our game. Apparently, several of their players were quoted by Nebraska papers as predicting an upset against us. I don't read the sports pages much during the season, but apparently our players did. Some of them took offense at some of the quotes attributed to

Washington State players. The game was played with great intensity on both sides of the ball.

Tommie Frazier played another excellent game. He ran for two touchdowns and threw for another. He even made a great block on a reverse by Clester Johnson. Although Ahman Green didn't start the game, he still gained 176 yards on only 13 carries.

We did allow them to score on an 87-yard touchdown run early in the game, but our defense settled down and played very well throughout the remainder of the game, except for a late touchdown against our second-string players. The final score was 35-21, a little closer than we would have liked. However, our performance was generally solid. Although Washington State went downhill later on in the year, they were playing good football when we met them.

Oddly enough, this was the first time Nebraska had beaten Washington State. We were 0-3 against them over the years. I still remember the game we lost to them in Lincoln in the mid-1970s. We had an excellent football team but they upset us. They were coached by Warren Powers, one of our former assistant coaches. Warren prepared them well, but we gave them some help, too, when we missed several scoring opportunities. That loss against Washington State was one of the most disappointing during my coaching career at Nebraska. So we especially appreciated the victory this time around.

11

A MUCH NEEDED
OPEN DATE

We had an open date on October 7, and it came at an excellent time. Brook Berringer suffered what appeared to be a slight bruise on his knee late in the game with Washington State. The knee continued to swell and eventually the swelling went down into his calf and his ankle. We assumed the injury was to a bursa sac that, when injured, usually fills with clear fluid. However, it soon became obvious that he was hemorrhaging in the knee. The bleeding had spread to the point where his whole thigh, knee, calf and ankle turned purple.

Brook wasn't the only player who would have been unable to play had a game been scheduled. Phil Ellis had broken a bone in his foot during practice. Phil had been starting for us at middle linebacker and had been playing very well, so we were uneasy about losing him for several weeks. Our starting offensive left tackle, Chris Dishman, had come down with pneumonia and would have been very doubtful to play. We also had both of our starting offensive guards, Steve Ott and Aaron Taylor, down with badly sprained ankles. It's possible they could have played, but they couldn't have played at their best. In addition, Kenny Cheatham, one of our top receivers, fell on his shoulder in practice and separated it.

I'm always uneasy when we have an open date. Coaches are usually tempted to add too much offensive and defensive strategy for the next game because of the extra time to prepare. In the past, we've also struggled to find the right balance for keeping the players sharp, yet not overworking them during practice. We had some hard practices but then gave the players Saturday and Sunday off. I think it's always helpful to give the players two days away from football during an open date. The physical fatigue and the injuries begin to increase toward the middle of the season, but the mental and emotional fatigue is even greater. So while an open date can create coaching problems, it does give our players a break from a long season.

An NCAA rule that I think is important is one that requires colleges to provide the players with a day off from football each week. Although we have been giving our players a day off for many years, there are still some schools that have players lift, run and study film on Sundays. This is supposedly "voluntary." But if they don't do the "voluntary" session, then they're required to make up this session Monday morning or evening. I'm convinced this extra session is not only counterproductive, but also borders on breaking NCAA rules.

A rule limiting practice and meeting time to 20 hours a week is also a good one. When the rule was first implemented, we found that we were only spending 18 to 19 hours a week to prepare for a game anyway. Although it wasn't a problem for us to adjust to the new rule, many schools were practicing their players much longer. Some were spending 30 to 35 hours a week in preparation. Obviously, it's difficult for an athlete to concentrate on his studies when giving so much time to football.

Lawrence Phillips continued to follow the guidelines we had given him following the assault on the victim. He was seeing a counselor at the Student Health Center twice a week and was also seeing a psychiatrist once a week. He was attending class regularly and was fulfilling all of the demands placed upon him by me, the university and the courts.

Some were now suggesting that I wouldn't permanently suspend a player, no matter what he did. This is not true. Since the previous spring I had dismissed three players from our team. In each case the player was given the same opportunity that Lawrence had been given. They were warned that they were not meeting certain expectations. Then they were given a set of procedures to follow if they wanted to stay on the football team. These players didn't follow through on what was required of them and were permanently suspended. One player had exceptional talent and probably would have played later in the NFL. Another player wouldn't have played much during '95, but would have contributed to our team the following two years. The third player wouldn't have played much for us at any time.

I dismissed our first-string I-back during the summer of '91. He had not been doing the things that we had expected of him as a student or athlete. Since he didn't meet the guidelines he was given to help him get back on track, we removed him from the team. That year we had less depth at I-back than during the '95 season. The dismissed player had a lot of potential and probably would have been a high draft pick in the NFL.

When I assessed the progress of our team at this point in the season, I was quite pleased. Although we were only at mid-season, our progress was remarkable. We had two linebackers surface in the early part of the season who were beginning to make an impact. Terrell Farley became a starter at weakside linebacker. Though he was a recent junior college transfer, he picked up things quickly. Because of his excellent instincts and speed it was almost like having another defensive back on the field. Jamel Williams was also beginning to emerge at the strongside linebacker position opposite Terrell Farley. In high school he had been a running back, so it wasn't too surprising that he had outstanding speed and agility. He also had excellent pass coverage skills. Jay Foreman had been starting at the strongside linebacker as a redshirt freshman. He continued to play well, particularly against the run. Ryan Terwilliger had been starting at weakside linebacker ahead of Terrell Farley and was a solid player. This gave us excellent depth at the linebacker positions—especially with our two fine backers in the middle, Phil Ellis and Doug Colman.

Mike Fullman, a transfer player from Rutgers, had begun to emerge as an excellent punt returner. Our secondary was playing solid football and was allowing fewer big plays. We were also getting an excellent pass rush from our two rush ends, Jared Tomich and Grant Wistrom. They were perhaps the best pair of rush ends we've had at Nebraska. I was also pleased with the progress of true freshman Chad Kelsay. He was our third rush end, and although he was from a small town in Nebraska, he had made tremendous progress. The Peter brothers, Jason and Christian, were nearly impossible to knock off the ball at defensive tackle so our inside play was solid.

Offensively, the line had exceeded expectations. They worked extremely well together as a unit. Our receivers were tenacious blockers. Players like Jon Vedral, Brendan Holbein and Clester Johnson did a tremendous job of blocking downfield for us.

Although our depth at I-back had dwindled, Ahman Green had really given us the support we needed from this critical position. We were also quite pleased with the play of our fullbacks, Jeff Makovicka, Brian Schuster and Joel Makovicka. All three were walk-ons from small Nebraska towns. The Makovicka brothers played eight-man football in high school.

Of course, Frazier and Berringer were playing very well. And Matt Turman was a very good third quarterback. Our freshman kicker, Kris Brown, took over his responsibilities better than anyone could have predicted. Jesse Kosch was also punting well.

Obviously, I was very pleased with the way things had gone on the field. We were poised to make another run at a Big Eight title and I felt good about our chances.

However, we had our work cut out for us. We were scheduled to play the University of Colorado, University of Kansas and Kansas State. They were all undefeated and ranked in the top 10 at that point in the season. And of course, we had to play our longtime rival, the University of Oklahoma. They were 4-1 and appeared to have a very strong football team as well.

Our next opponent, the University of Missouri, had been struggling throughout most of the season, so while preparing for our game they closed their practices to make some changes. It was rumored that they were going to start a different quarterback.

Since they had gone six quarters without a touchdown and were 2-4 overall and 0-2 in the Big Eight, I was sure they were willing to take some chances to turn their season around.

Their surprise was freshman quarterback Corby Jones. They pulled him out of his redshirt year and installed some option football because he was a good runner. However, our defense played very well and we posted our first shutout of the season. We held Missouri to 122 total yards.

Tommie Frazier had a great day against Missouri. He ran for three touchdowns and passed for two more. This broke the Nebraska career record for touchdowns. Offensively we had 475 total yards, which was the fewest yards for one game during the season. However, because we often had good field position during the game, it took fewer yards to score. We capitalized on nearly every scoring opportunity in our 57-0 victory.

Ahman Green started his first game against Missouri and ran for 90 yards on 15 carries. Terrell Farley also had his first start of the season at linebacker and contributed to our kicking game as well when he blocked a punt for a safety.

Offensively we played without a turnover. At times, we didn't play with much intensity, but it was a very solid performance. I was confident that we were going to improve as we moved into the tough part of our schedule. Our next game against Kansas State figured to be a challenge. Soon we would find out just how good we were.

12

A CRUCIAL GAME

Friday before the Missouri game, we were confronted by an unusual situation. I was told about the Million Man March, which was to be held the following Monday, October 17. It was to be held in Washington D.C. and was led by Louis Farrakhan of the Nation of Islam. Many African-American men around the country were urged to participate in the march or stay home from work. A few days before the march, a spokesman from the Nation of Islam urged our African-American players not to practice on the following Monday.

Fortunately, I heard about the possible conflict between our practice and the march. When I talked to our players about the march, I explained the importance of our upcoming Kansas State game. I wanted to be sensitive to the needs of the African-American players, but I wasn't willing to sacrifice any of the four days of practice we needed to prepare for the game. I figured we could practice Sunday afternoon and take Monday off. Then we could resume our practice schedule on Tuesday so we wouldn't miss any practice days. However, if there were only a few African-American players who chose not to practice on Monday, then we would go ahead with our regular practice schedule.

When I asked if any players wanted to be excused from practice during the march, only one player said he would rather not. Therefore, I told the team we would take Sunday off as usual and practice Monday.

I also asked our players to let me know if they felt I hadn't treated them fairly. I didn't want to cause any racial tension because of my decision to practice during the march. I invited any players with concerns about this matter to attend the Unity Council meeting on the following Tuesday evening. None of our players expressed any problems with the situation. The march could have led to a difficult situation; however, I thought that the players handled it well.

I'm opposed to any group or movement that promotes separation. Athletics has been one area where racial and socioeconomic barriers have broken down more quickly than in most other parts of our society. Our coaches and players work hard at promoting racial harmony and understanding on our team.

As our team resumed preparation for Kansas State, Lawrence Phillips remained suspended. Lawrence's season became even stranger when he called a talk show. After listening to an Omaha talk show that was discussing his situation, he surprised everyone by calling the show himself. I'm sure he was frustrated by the comments of the uninformed callers. Since he hadn't spoken publicly about the case, his comments became instant news at every media outlet in Nebraska—if not the country.

Lawrence told the radio listeners that he had received offers to sign with several agents for as much as $100,000. All he needed to do was sign the contract and simply "hang out" in either California or Florida until the pro draft. He said that he declined the offers because signing with an agent would only show a weakness in his character. He also talked about how his goal in '95 was to win the Heisman Trophy. Now he was interested in possibly trying to win it again in '96. He also made it clear that he didn't want to return to Nebraska in '96 if the fans were not in favor of his return. Finally, he talked about his desire to overcome his anger problem and return to the team to finish the season.

I think the personal call made Lawrence more real to many fans. Often when people see a football player, they only see an indestructible robot. They forget there is a human being behind the face mask. Our players have the same feelings and aspirations as anyone else. I'm sure Lawrence's phone call helped many fans understand that he was a young man who made a mistake, but he was still a human being.

I announced at the press conference prior to the Kansas State game that Lawrence would not play against Kansas State or Colorado. Both teams were ranked high nationally and were the strongest teams on our schedule. I hoped most people knew I wouldn't bring Lawrence back on the team just to win another Big Eight Championship or a national championship. However, some simply didn't want Lawrence back on the team, period. I think they felt if he were reinstated on the team it wouldn't send the "right message."

Kansas State was undefeated and ranked No. 8, when we prepared to play them. Obviously, it was a big game, and Bill Snyder had done an excellent coaching job. When Bill took over at Kansas State, they had one of the worst records in Division I football. Because of his dedication to the program and attention to detail, Bill had turned Kansas State into an outstanding football team.

Kansas State's defensive coordinator, Bobby Stoops is also a great football coach whom I respect. When you play Kansas State, you know they are going take away some of the things you do best on offense. We have to be flexible and go with whatever their defensive scheme allows us to do. Offensively they always have a fine thrower and great receivers. We would need to play well on both sides of the ball.

We got off to a great start early in the game when Mike Fullman returned a punt 79 yards for a touchdown. This was our first punt return for a score since 1988. Mike benefited from a great block thrown by Mike Rucker who hit a Kansas State player so hard he knocked off his helmet. The return was great until Mike decided to high step his way into the end zone. He was flagged for celebrating his touchdown. The penalty for celebrating had been reinterpreted and was enforced rigorously in 1995 in an effort to eliminate unsportsmanlike displays. Some argued the rule took some of the spontaneity out of the game. We were disappointed that Mike didn't heed our warnings about such displays, but were also very glad that he scored.

Kansas State capitalized on the 15-yard celebration penalty on the ensuing kickoff to generate a drive that led to a score. Although we came back to score again, we only had a 14-6 lead at the end of the quarter. We scored three more times in the second quarter. Two touchdowns were on passes from Tommie Frazier.

The third was a spectacular play where Grant Wistrom deflected a shovel pass into the hands of our other rush end, Luther Hardin, who scored from three yards out. Later, Frazier threw another touchdown pass to Jon Vedral that made the score 42-6. It looked like the game was pretty well over, and our coaches started thinking ahead to the upcoming Colorado game. Even though we had almost an entire quarter of football remaining, we began to substitute our players freely in order to rest our top players and protect them from injury. This almost led to disaster.

Kansas State responded by scoring three straight times in the fourth quarter. They ran two fake punts on fourth down that set up touchdowns. Then they blocked a punt for a touchdown. We had put our second-string punt team in, had a breakdown in our blocking and got the punt blocked.

Suddenly the game was 42-25. With almost six minutes remaining in the game, I was upset with the prospect of putting our first units back in the game to secure the win. Once out of the game, players relax mentally and are often more subject to injury if put back in.

We went ahead and put our top units back in the game. Our offense generated a good drive capped by a 12-yard shovel pass from Tommie Frazier to Ahman Green. Ahman was hit short of the goal line and showed tremendous balance and strength as he lunged into the end zone for the clinching touchdown. Unfortunately, he suffered a severely sprained ankle in the process. He was helped off the field. I thought he would probably not be able to play against Colorado the following week because he couldn't put weight on the ankle.

As I walked off the field, I was gratified by the way our team had played. But at the same time I was kicking myself for being forced to put our first team back in the game. We were already short of I-backs, so it was unfortunate to lose Ahman in the process. I was afraid we might have blown the Colorado game by trying to preserve the win against Kansas State.

Kansas State was ranked No. 1 in total defense nationally before our game. They held us to only 338 yards total offense. However, we had the ball for only 63 plays and had good field position most of the time. This meant scoring drives were shorter so we didn't have to generate as much yardage. We had to rely more on our passing game than usual. Tommie Frazier's four touchdown passes certainly made the margin of victory more comfortable.

Defensively we played well, particularly against the K-State running game. We sacked their quarterback nine times. Eventually their quarterback, Matt Miller, had to leave the game because of the beating he had taken from our pass rush. Kansas State had minus-19 yards on the ground, though they did throw for 275 yards.

Monday, October 23, the university ruled that Lawrence Phillips would not be expelled from school. I was pleased with the way Jim Griesen, our Vice Chancellor for Student Affairs, and Linda Schwartzkopf, Director of Student Judicial Affairs, handled the situation. I know there was a lot of pressure to expel Lawrence from school from different special interest groups.

Jim and Linda probably had the most accurate picture of what happened the night of the assault. They talked extensively to Lawrence, to the victim, to Scott Frost and to other witnesses who were in the apartment building during the assault.

I felt both Jim and Linda examined the facts and based their ruling on similar student cases. Our chancellor, Joan Leitzel, was also fair in the way she approached the issue. I'm sure she also received a great deal of pressure to get rid of Lawrence.

Our athletic director, Bill Byrne, did a good job of dealing with Lawrence and the victim. He insisted on following the proper procedures for protecting the victim, yet he was also fair to Lawrence. From the administrative side, I could not have asked for a more exhaustive yet fair examination of the matter.

Ultimately, the decision to play Lawrence came back to me. The administration could have taken it out of my hands by expelling Lawrence or ruling that he couldn't play. When I talked to Lawrence, I could see that he had gained some maturity and insight into his problem. Although I wasn't absolutely certain how he would react if given a chance to play again, I thought there was a good chance that it would have a positive effect on his behavior.

There were more reporters than normal at our Tuesday noon press conference. While I'm sure part of the interest was because we were going to play Colorado, many reporters came to hear my announcement about Lawrence Phillips' status.

Before the press conference I had previously met with Chancellor Leitzel, Bill Byrne and Jim Griesen regarding how information concerning Lawrence's case would be released to the media. We had examined all the factors concerning Lawrence's case. A significant part of our previous review concerned the Menninger report done on Lawrence. With Lawrence's permission I include several key parts of the report:

(1) There was no psychotic or neurological disorder that rendered him dangerous to himself or others. The report stated:

"There was no level of a psychotic level of organization to his thinking."

Also, Dr. Daniel Katz, neurologist, found no neurological abnormalities.

(2) His previous experiences made close relationships difficult, yet Lawrence didn't appear to be a serious threat to the victim and didn't appear to be one who had a significant problem with control. The report said:

"The results of the psychological testing do not suggest an individual for whom uncontrolled aggression is an ongoing problem . . . this young man is quite aware of what has happened and the consequences of his actions and does appear to feel remorseful about them. The incident in question was a severe stressor for Mr. Phillips who has suffered a significant personal loss. He makes it clear that he holds no malice toward his former girlfriend and does not want to harm her in any way. Specifically, his experience of childhood was that he was never quite good enough to keep the people he needed around him. His father left him and was absent from the time Mr. Phillips was quite young and his mother, while available for a number of years, when Mr. Phillips was age 12, was involved with another man. The patient developed a sense that something was innately wrong with him and that he was 'messed up' and, as a result, other people would not be there for him. The incident with his girlfriend led unfortunately to yet another loss of a significant person in his life."

(3) Lawrence was diagnosed as having an "adjustment disorder."

"Adjustment disorder is not related to anxiety or a mood disorder. The stressor indeed was felt to be a single event; namely, the termination of a romantic relationship but in the context of the social situation which has been described in this report."

(4) It was recommended that Lawrence enter into therapy.

"The results of this evaluation strongly suggest a need for this individual to be in some form of psychotherapy. It was also felt that a combination of individual psychotherapy and group psychotherapy could be particularly helpful to him."

(5) It was not recommended that Lawrence be put on medication.

"He does not abuse alcohol or drugs, and this does not seem to be a problem for him. He is not felt to be a good candidate for medication at the present time."

(6) The issue of football was addressed and it was stated that football could be an important part of his recovery.

"With regard to his ability to play football, while playing football is a mixed bag for him in that it is both quite stressful and quite rewarding; to not play would be psychologically difficult for him as this is such an important component of his identity and self-esteem. Again, I think that what will be most important psychologically for this man is not to prevent him from doing those things which he is able to do well and from which he can gain a considerable amount of self-esteem and positive responses from others but to add to that some additional activities such as psychotherapy which will allow him to balance out his activities so that everything doesn't rest in one or two situations."

Obviously, Lawrence's family history and his sense of abandonment was intensified by the loss of his girlfriend. Two other sources of stress for Lawrence were not referred to in the report. First, at the time of the assault Lawrence had been under a great deal of scrutiny and was uncertain from day to day about his playing status due to the NCAA investigation into his relationship with the agent. Second, Lawrence was worried about his mother, who had lost her job. Although she was far away from him, she still seemed to be a major concern in his life.

Nothing in the report suggested that Lawrence couldn't resume a normal life with the help of psychotherapy and a structured environment, particularly the structure provided by football. Since football was very important to him, it wouldn't have made sense to take away another thing that provided him with much needed self-esteem.

Lawrence cooperated fully when he entered counseling with John Goldrich, an African-American counselor who works in our Student Health Center. I observed several noticeable changes in Lawrence's attitude toward his teammates and others. I'm certain his change in attitude was at least partially due to the counseling. He also continued to receive help from Dr. Boman Bastani, his psychiatrist. Lawrence continued to comply with the other areas of his treatment such as going to class regularly and avoiding any contact with the victim.

Lawrence showed he was willing to take responsibility for his misconduct. He admitted his problem and I believe he was sincerely sorry for what he did. I know he also felt badly for how the assault affected the football program. Most of us felt it would be best if he didn't play against Colorado. Otherwise, we felt people would think he was only returning to win football games. For that reason, we decided to let him practice while preparing for Colorado, but not to allow him to play until Iowa State a week later. Unfortunately, no matter what game he returned for, there would be those who claimed that he was brought back just so we could win.

It would have been easier for the university, the athletic department and me to have kept Lawrence off the team. I'm sure the special interest groups would have applauded us if we had done so. In their minds, this would have sent a message to other men who might commit violent acts against women. However, I knew I couldn't live with myself if I allowed others to pressure me into a decision that I didn't think was right.

The university administration involved itself fully in decisions regarding Lawrence Phillips. I made no decision about his return to the football team until after the Student Judicial Process had completed its deliberations and decided on appropriate sanctions. After that, I greatly appreciated and respected the administration for allowing me to decide if Lawrence should be allowed to play football. Later, Joan Leitzel said, "We did the right thing."

Although very well qualified, Joan was not selected as a finalist for the Chancellor's position at UNL though she had performed admirably in that job as acting chancellor. She was a person of integrity and considerable fortitude. I was afraid that the Lawrence Phillips decision might have damaged her position with the search committee, and I hope that her involvement with Lawrence's case didn't work against her. In March of 1996, Joan was named President at the University of New Hampshire—she will be missed in Lincoln by those of us who worked with her.

We all knew that the decision to play Lawrence would bring another onslaught from the media. However, those involved in the decision were willing to pay the price. I could only hope that Lawrence would follow through on his treatment and would make the best of a difficult situation.

On Monday, October 23, Lawrence returned to practice. I told the press he wouldn't play against Colorado. Although he would not be the starter, he would play a week later against Iowa State. Lawrence's biggest problem once he returned to practice was no longer the press, but trying to get back in shape. He had been away from football for nearly six weeks. He worked hard in practice, but the extra weight he had gained during his layoff had slowed him down. I knew he wouldn't be in top form for several weeks.

As we prepared for Colorado, we were terribly short at I-back. Damon Benning reinjured a hamstring in practice and was unable to practice early in the week. Ahman Green was still hobbling from the ankle sprain that he suffered against Kansas State. He didn't practice on Monday and wasn't able to finish practice on Tuesday. James Sims was still healthy, but while he was running a pass pattern, he was accidentally blindsided by a player who was involved in another drill. Unfortunately, he suffered a hip pointer that looked as though it might keep him out of the game. He had to be helped off the practice field. As a result, Clinton Childs was the only reasonably healthy I-back we had left. But even he was suffering from a sore shoulder. It seems that when injuries come, they come in clusters. I couldn't remember having so many I-backs hurt. If winning was the only thing that mattered to our program we would have surely played Lawrence against Colorado.

Before we left for Boulder, I told Lawrence it was too bad he couldn't play. But he responded by assuring me that we didn't have anything to worry about. I wasn't nearly as confident as he was. To me, it looked like a tough game because we were going to play a very good team on the road. Colorado had an excellent offensive line and some great receivers. They lost Koy Detmer, their starting quarterback, earlier in the year to a knee injury. But John Hessler, who replaced him, had a good arm and could run well. Colorado had been upset by Kansas earlier in the season; therefore, we knew our game was even more important to them.

Colorado's new coach, Rick Neuheisel, was taking a different approach to the Nebraska game than his predecessor, Bill McCartney. I've always respected Bill as a football coach and as a person, but I could never understand the need to make Nebraska a "rival." I know Bill himself wasn't responsible for the Nebraska jokes on the radio the week before we played. And he couldn't be blamed for all of the animosity between the fans in recent years. However, the so-called rivalry was surrounded by too much hostility. I was glad to hear Rick Neuheisel downplay the importance of the "rivalry."

I did have second thoughts about his remarks as we warmed up for the game. Maybe it wasn't just another game, as he stated. I noticed their players and coaches during their warm up leave the field about 15 minutes earlier than normal. I assumed something unusual might happen. While we were in the locker room, I was told their entire team walked down through the stands with one of their players beating on drums to arouse their fans. I had seen Colorado use nearly every type of technique to motivate their players, but this was definitely new.

The Colorado mascot, a buffalo named Ralphie, is escorted around the field before the game. Just prior to the kickoff, Ralphie and her handlers came running right down the sideline on our side of the field. I motioned for the handlers to steer Ralphie out further on the field, but they came so close they barely missed us on the sideline. Someday Ralphie is going to cream somebody.

I've always believed that pregame emotion doesn't carry very far into a game. On our first play from scrimmage we pitched the ball to Ahman Green who ran 57 yards for a touchdown. Because we had lined up in a new formation, a full-house backfield with two split ends, Colorado was confused. All we needed was an extra blocker in front of Ahman to allow him to use his exceptional speed to beat everyone down the sideline. Fortunately, Ahman had improved each day throughout the week as his ankle got stronger, so he was able to start the game.

The play was reminiscent of a screen pass we opened the game with in Colorado in 1989. On that play we threw the ball to our fullback, Bryan Carpenter, who scored on the first play of the game. Although it was an emotional lift, we still lost that game because of two long punt returns against us. I'm always concerned about scoring too easily and quickly during a game. Sometimes this means your players will relax mentally and lose their concentration. However, there wasn't any reason to worry because we continued to give a great effort throughout the game.

Tommie Frazier had another great game as he rushed for 40 yards and added 241 yards passing while throwing for two touchdowns. For me, the most memorable play of the game was when Tommie got blindsided by their linebacker Mike Phillips. Tommie was still able to take the hit and release the football with enough velocity to get the pass to Ahman Green, who gained 35 yards along the west sideline. Later, Tommie led an 83-yard scoring drive as time was running out in the first half. It was climaxed with a 7-yard touchdown pass to Jon Vedral with 10 seconds remaining. The drive nearly guaranteed a win, since it put us up 31-14.

It was a remarkable game because we had no penalty yards for the first time since 1976. We also had no turnovers for the third straight game. Another statistic that was amazing was that we had no sacks. In fact, we had no sacks for the entire season. Kris Brown continued to kick well as he made all three of his field-goal attempts and was five-for-five on extra points. All coaches like to know they can depend on their kicker to be consistent, particularly in big games.

Although we allowed Colorado to complete some passes, our defense managed two interceptions. Our pass rush was good and generally we covered their speedy receivers well. One interception was caused when Hessler was hit by Grant Wistrom as he attempted to pass and Doug Colman intercepted the ball. We played more zone coverage in this ballgame than we had played in previous games. At times, I think this kept their quarterback off-balance.

We scored 10 points in the fourth quarter. Kris Brown kicked a 37-yard field goal and Frazier ran two yards for a touchdown with a little less than three minutes remaining to seal the victory. The final score was 44-21. After the game, I thought we had a good chance to be ranked No. 1. Tommie Frazier's performance gave him a chance to win the Heisman Trophy because the game was televised in most parts of the country.

I was amazed at how well we played in a noisy and hostile

environment. For our players to execute as well as they did, showed remarkable concentration.

Following the game, we had a final reminder that this was no ordinary football game. While traveling to the airport, three young men chose to make obscene gestures at our bus, once they recognized who we were. One of them seemed to go berserk when he saw the team bus and exposed himself through the car window on the interstate. We took down the license number and description of the car and called the Colorado highway patrol on a cellular phone. Whether the Colorado police did anything to the young men, I'm not sure. But their behavior does show how distorted people's values can be. This "fan" obviously didn't appreciate the effort and sacrifice made by players on both teams.

We had an interesting speaker at our chapel service prior to that game. Derek Fullmer was a former Colorado football player and is a current Fellowship of Christian Athletes staff member in Colorado. He presented the gospel clearly to our players. Derek did a great job of dispelling any notion that he was partisan. He genuinely admired our team and cared for our players. It was our common belief in Christ that bonded us together. I sensed that the University of Colorado has many players who are spiritually committed. I'm sure this has kept the atmosphere around the game from getting out of control. A large number of Nebraska and Colorado players and coaches gathered on the field for a postgame prayer. This was something that I don't believe was reported by the press.

Many fans don't understand how two teams can knock each other around for a couple of hours and still respect one another once the game is over. There is usually little or no animosity between the players as they walk off the field. They know what kind of effort the opponent has given to prepare for and to play the game, and they can empathize with how their opponents may be feeling. There have been very few occasions where I have felt any hostility toward rival coaches or players at the conclusion of a game. I'm usually tired and my emotions generally revolve around how well I feel our team has played.

13

ENCOUNTERING THE NATIONAL NEWS

Following the Colorado game, I noticed a letter to the editor in a local paper that asked "Would Tom Osborne allow Lawrence Phillips to play on the football team if his daughter had been the victim of the attack instead of someone else?" When I read the letter I was angry at first because I thought the question was so personal. But after thinking about it, I knew my answer to the question would be "yes."

Permanently dismissing Lawrence from the football team wouldn't have helped any of my family members or anyone else's family. If anything, it might have made things worse. By not getting the needed treatment, something similar may have happened in the future. At least if he were on the team, I could make sure he would get the help he needed.

Recently, several professional athletes have been charged with assault. None of them, as far as I know, were suspended for the season or even for a game. I'm sure that some were not even required to undergo counseling. In comparison, Lawrence did not get off easily. Lawrence had missed most of the season, had undergone counseling, and would probably suffer financially by being taken later in the NFL draft.

Things didn't get much better for Lawrence. On Halloween day he sprained his ankle in practice. Christian Peter, one of our starting defensive linemen, suffered a severe knee strain and was questionable for the Iowa State game. Jared Tomich, one of our top rush ends, was nursing a bad back and would probably not play.

At our regularly scheduled Tuesday noon press conference, I met with members of the media to discuss the upcoming Iowa State game. Unexpectedly, a member of the press, Bernard Goldberg, broke in and asked, "Coach, I understand this may not be the most popular subject to bring up in Lincoln, but let me try anyway. If one of your players had roughed up a member of your family and then dragged her down a flight of steps—" I didn't let him finish. I didn't think he sincerely wanted to know my answer. Instead I thought he was a reporter trying to get a particular response from me.

I resented his asking the question as I was in the middle of discussing the upcoming Iowa State game. I had read the same question in the letters to the editor section a few days before, so I suspected he was simply repeating it. I asked him where he was from. He said he was from CBS News, and then he went on to say, "Would you have reinstated that player on your team?" I replied, "I'm not going to talk about that, okay? And I kind of resent that question, to be very honest with you." Goldberg responded, "Can you tell me why?" and I said "Yes, but I don't think this is the right place or time. If you want to talk in the hall, I'll talk." By now I was really angry, but I managed to keep from totally losing my temper and answered a few questions local reporters asked. When I left the press conference, I went out in the hallway and Goldberg was waiting for me with a camera man. I asked them to turn off the camera and answered Goldberg's question. I told him I would play Lawrence even if he assaulted a member of my family. Then I quickly walked away.

Apparently, Goldberg's purpose for asking the question was to get some type of dramatic response from me that he could use on CBS's "Eye on America" broadcast. During this regular feature of CBS News, Bernard Goldberg asked the question, "America, are athletes allowed to play the game of life by a different set of rules?" In the broadcast, Goldberg and CBS News implied that Lawrence Phillips was being allowed to play so Nebraska could win a national championship. They claimed a football program like Nebraska was only concerned with money. While trying to make their point, they made several inaccurate statements.

Goldberg said, "Nebraska would pick up $8 million just for being invited to the Fiesta Bowl." Actually, Nebraska would only get one-eighth of the Fiesta Bowl payout. Instead of receiving $8 million as Goldberg said, we received one-eighth of a total of $10.5 million, minus $1.5 million for travel expenses. After expenses, we received slightly more than one million from our share of the Fiesta Bowl profits. Chris Anderson, our Sports Information Director, told CBS the $8 million figure was inaccurate, but they still reported it.

Next, Goldberg, said "Receiver Riley Washington is accused of attempted second-degree murder on this convenience store clerk." A photo of Jermaine Cole was shown at that point. Jermaine Cole was not a convenience store clerk. It seemed that Goldberg was implying that Riley was involved in a holdup. Rather than being an innocent store clerk, Jermaine Cole had numerous arrests and was not an employee at the Kwik Shop.

CBS News had Madeline Popa appear on camera questioning my ethics. She said I was only interested in winning. Popa was not identified by CBS, so viewers got the impression that she was a typical fan in Lincoln. Actually, she was the state coordinator of the National Organization for Women and had been a very outspoken critic of Lawrence Phillips being allowed to play.

Goldberg said Lawrence dragged the victim down the flight of steps, threw her into a mailbox, and left her lying on the floor bleeding from the head. The evidence does not show that the victim was thrown into the mailboxes. Instead the damage to the mailboxes was done by Lawrence's fists.

The CBS newscast identified five players who had been in trouble. However, the story misled viewers into thinking all of the players' problems happened recently. But the facts were much different. Not mentioned in the newscast were the facts that the incidents happened during the last four years and that four of the players were suspended from the team. Each player was disciplined according to a set code of conduct for our football team.

CBS never asked to talk with me. I had been available to the press for at least six weeks concerning Lawrence Phillips. It seemed obvious to me that CBS already knew what they wanted to report and were only gathering facts that fit their story. I felt badly that they would not have at least tried to talk to me before they told the world that I was operating from motives that were self-serving.

I thought their theory that I was playing Lawrence simply to get to the Fiesta Bowl was irrational. After all, if this was the case, why would we have kept Lawrence benched for six games and especially for two of our most difficult games, Kansas State and Colorado? When we played Colorado, we really needed Lawrence because of the injuries to our I-backs. However, we didn't back away from the stated rehabilitation schedule we had set up and Lawrence didn't play.

Goldberg, unlike other television reporters, had a camera and microphone on himself as well as having a camera on me. This procedure was not new to CBS News. It is my understanding that CBS had previously used the routine on people such as General William Westmoreland, George Bush and other individuals who were in the news. I should have been quite honored to have been included in that company. Having two cameras allows the reporter to be shown asking his question while the other camera records the response or reaction.

Goldberg said, "Winning is what big-time college sports is all about—winning and money," implying that Nebraska only cared about winning football games and making money. It was anything but a balanced piece on Nebraska. CBS didn't bother to mention that Nebraska had an excellent academic record. Our football graduation rate was the highest of any Big Eight school this past year and was in the top 10 percent of all College Football Association schools. We have had more Academic All-Americans than any football program in the nation. We have had no major sanctions from the NCAA over the past 34 years. Usually, a "win-at-all-cost" program will have some major rules violations during that many years. Our teams have never been involved in a major brawl or ruckus of any kind on the field. Our demeanor during games has usually been quite good. We are usually one of the least penalized teams in our league.

I was used to dealing with media types from the sports arena. I don't agree with everything they report, but in general find them to be people who do their homework and try to be fair. I can honestly say that there are very few sports reporters, local or national, that I don't like and get along with reasonably well. Dealing with reporters from the news side was a whole new ballgame. As Marlin Fitzwater states in his book *Call the Briefing,* "As in any gunfight, it's hard to win when the other guy is wearing a bullet-proof vest. In any case, the press can never be destroyed. They determine their own condition. Winning means convincing the press to let you live." I could see what Fitzwater was talking about.

I was interested in an article that recently appeared in the *Wall Street Journal.* The article starts by saying: "There are lots of reasons fewer people are watching network news, and one of them, I'm more convinced than ever, is that our viewers simply don't trust us. And for good reason.

"The old argument that the networks and other 'media elites' have a liberal bias is so blatantly true that it's hardly worth discussing anymore. No, we don't sit around in dark corners and plan strategies on how we're going to slant the news. We don't have to. It comes naturally to us." The author? Bernard Goldberg.

I don't dislike Bernard Goldberg. I don't even know him. I'm sorry that he works in an arena that is so competitive that he says slanting the news comes naturally.

Westinghouse bought CBS not long after the Bernard Goldberg interview was aired. According to newspaper reports,

CBS News was rated last among major news programs when it was purchased. The new owners were interested in improving CBS News ratings. I hope they begin by emphasizing accuracy and balance.

Once we decided to let Lawrence rejoin the team, it provoked all kinds of responses. Some letters I received were negative and filled with hate. The most threatening letters were turned over to the police. Several of them threatened my life and sometimes my family. Nearly all of the threatening letters mentioned O.J. Simpson as well. Somehow O. J. Simpson was closely linked in the minds of some people with Lawrence Phillips. A writer from Boston even suggested I contact O.J. if I really needed a running back.

I'm sure much of the emotion surrounding the Phillips' case was an outgrowth of the feelings some had about O. J. Simpson and his murder trial. Unfortunately, many of them couldn't make the distinction between the two.

About this time, a Lincoln psychiatrist was quoted as saying, "Tom Osborne's ethical compass has a needle that is turning back and forth." He seemed to imply that I was only doing what was expedient. I thought it was odd that he made this statement. He knew me personally, so he must have known that I dealt with Lawrence Phillips in the same way I dealt with Scott Baldwin, a player who played for us a few years ago. Scott's case was widely publicized in Lincoln, so I couldn't understand how he could be surprised by the way I dealt with Lawrence.

Scott had once been our starting I-back, but several injuries slowed him down. During the winter of '92, he had a mental breakdown and attacked a young woman who was walking her dog. The woman was injured so badly we weren't sure if she would survive. Because of a head injury, it was a long time before we knew if she would ever be normal again.

Scott was eventually found to have been not guilty due to insanity. As part of his court order, Scott was released on the condition that he not live by himself. He was required to live either with me, our backfield coach, Frank Solich, or the Reverend Donald Coleman. He spent roughly two months living with each of us. He was also instructed to stay on his medication, which enabled him to live a normal life. After being released from our supervision, Scott stopped taking his medicine, which resulted in another psychotic episode in Omaha. When two female police officers attempted to arrest him, he was shot after a tragic chain of events. Because of the shooting, he was paralyzed from the waist down.

After his paralysis, Frank Solich and I continued to visit him in the hospital and later in the Lincoln Regional Center. We made sure the athletic department continued to provide financial, academic and emotional support. Eventually he graduated from college. With the help of a young lady, Jolene Davidson, who has been tremendously supportive, Scott is leading a reasonably normal life. He is employed in Lincoln and plans to be married.

Our football program endured a great deal of public criticism for standing by Scott and helping him. We also did what we could for the victim, Gina Simanek. We visited her in the hospital and later at her rehabilitation home. We raised $35,000 to help defray her medical bills at our spring football game in 1992. Gina came to see me last summer. She seemed to have recovered well and told me she plans to attend graduate school and work on her doctorate. We remained friends, yet many in the public didn't see how I could help Scott and be concerned about Gina.

We were consistent with the way we dealt with Scott and Lawrence. Although Scott could no longer play football, we continued to aid and support him. We did not abandon him when there was no longer any possibility that he could help our team. I hope people also understand that we tried to do what was best for Lawrence as a human being and not simply to win football games.

In the meantime, we were getting ready for Iowa State. Lawrence was cleared to play and practices went well. We played perhaps our finest offensive football game of the season against Iowa State. We were nearly unstoppable. Ahman Green picked up 176 of our 624 rushing yards. Clinton Childs added another 70 yards. Tommie Frazier gained 62 yards on only 8 carries. In Lawrence's first game back, he gained 68 yards on 12 carries.

Iowa State's Troy Davis entered the game as the nation's leading rusher averaging 190 yards a game. He was also the fifth back in NCAA Division I-A history to rush for more than 2,000 yards in a season. We "held" him to 121 yards on 28 carries. He was definitely a great running back, but we also had a great defense against the run.

We added 152 yards passing to our 624 yards rushing, so we had a total of 776 yards. It was one of the best offensive performances ever by a Nebraska team.

Lawrence entered the game with about five minutes gone in the first quarter. He played well considering the long layoff due to the suspension. However, as I watched him sitting on the sidelines later in the game, I could tell he also knew he wasn't fully recovered from his layoff. Because he was such a great athlete, he could still perform well after only a few days of practice. However, he wasn't the same Lawrence Phillips. He had gained some weight, lost some speed, quickness and timing. I'm sure he was glad to be playing even if he wasn't at the top of his game.

The crowd was decent to Lawrence. I didn't hear any boos when he entered the game. There was simply a polite response to his return. I think the fans were letting Lawrence know they appreciated what he had been through and the courage it took to face his problems.

We played another game without a turnover and executed better than anyone could have predicted. We played nearly 100 players and scored only seven points in the fourth quarter, but the final score was 73-14. We scored on every offensive possession but one. It didn't make much difference who carried the ball, something good was going to happen when we had it.

14

A Slow Start and a Fast Finish in Kansas

Our momentum continued to build following the Iowa State game. We remained undefeated with a record of 9-0. Although we had a few injuries, we hadn't lost a starting player for any great length of time. It's rare for a team to be nearly injury-free after nine games. Unfortunately, the odds were about to catch up with us. While we prepared for the Kansas game, Tommie Frazier started to have problems in the same leg in which he had developed a blood clot 14 months earlier. Immediately, we had the vein in his leg examined for a recurrence of blood clots.

We were relieved when the doctors found that his vein was clear. Tommie must have bruised the lower part of his leg, which caused the swelling to drain into his ankle and foot. The swelling made it difficult for him to run or cut. Although he had to miss practice, he continued to improve to the point where I thought he might play. Tommie has a very high pain threshold. If there was any way that he could possibly perform, he certainly would.

However, we rely exclusively on medical opinion as to whether or not a player will be allowed to play. If a player risks permanent injury in playing, we will not allow him to play.

During the week before the Kansas game, Dennis Smith, the University of Nebraska president, was hospitalized to have an angioplasty procedure. Dennis had two blocked coronary arteries. Fortunately, the blockages were located where balloons could be inserted so that the blockages could be reopened. As I visited with Dennis, I was reminded of my own experience nearly 11 years ago. At that time I was diagnosed with a 95 percent blockage of the left anterior descending coronary artery. I underwent double bypass surgery to reroute the blood around the blockage. Neither Dennis nor I had any previous signs of heart disease.

I recall being 48 years old and being unsure about the risk factors for heart disease. There had been no reason for me to be concerned about heart disease. I wasn't overweight. I had never smoked, and exercise was part of my daily routine. I even thought my diet was fairly healthy. However, the biggest problem was my family history of cardiovascular disease. My father had a heart attack when he was 63 and eventually suffered a fatal one at 77. My mother suffered a stroke at age 72. Since I couldn't do much about my genetic background, I began to look for other ways to improve my health.

Most Americans don't have a very healthy diet, so I knew I should probably evaluate my own diet. Another concern was the coaching profession. It's a high stress occupation that many would say compounds coronary artery disease. For a while, I even considered leaving coaching. After thinking things over, I decided to make whatever changes were necessary to stay in coaching. It was a gamble but the prospect of life without football made the gamble seem worthwhile.

I was fortunate that my cardiologist, Dr. Walt Weaver, took an aggressive approach to changing my diet. He had spent more time researching the causes of coronary artery disease than most cardiologists at the time. Many cardiologists relied heavily on surgery, angioplasty or cholesterol-reducing pills to treat coronary artery disease. The result was often more surgery after a few years since many patients never changed their unhealthy lifestyles. Walt's approach was more focused on a permanent lifestyle change, particularly diet.

Since risk factors such as excess weight, lack of exercise and smoking were not problems, I decided to focus primarily on two areas that might make a difference, stress and diet.

It's not easy to control stress when you're a coach, but I did cut back on my schedule as much as I could. I was doing a weekly radio show, speaking at a weekly breakfast meeting in Omaha and serving as our offensive coordinator. Serving as the offensive coordinator involved many hours of film study so I could feel comfortable calling our plays. I also appeared at an Extra Point Luncheon on Mondays, did a television show on Sundays, had a noon press conference on Tuesdays and met with members of the press every day after practice.

I turned over some call-in radio show spots to assistants. We began to rotate the Monday Extra Point Luncheon among our staff. I reduced my early morning breakfast meetings in Omaha to three a year. The others were picked up by my assistants. I still had to do the press conferences and I continued to serve as the offensive coordinator. I'm convinced that stress and burnout occur when you try to do too many things you don't enjoy or don't have the talent to do. I tried to do more of those things I enjoyed and dropped several things I didn't. That's why I kept the offensive coordinator duties. I've always liked the offensive strategy involved in football. I simplified my life as much as I could and tried to focus on the activities that were most important.

I began to follow something called the Pritikin Diet. It was a very strict diet that allowed for only 10 percent or fewer calories from fat and practically no saturated fat. The average American diet is 40 to 50 percent fat and is quite high in saturated fat. This was an extreme diet and it was a real shock to my system. At the time there weren't too many foods in the supermarkets that were low in fat.

However, my wife Nancy, did her best to shop for food that fit my new diet. I felt badly that it took much more of her time to prepare our meals. I knew she must already have been worried about my ability to continue coaching, and now she must have been frustrated with my new diet.

My cardiologist had read several studies that showed people who ate a lot of cold water fish, such as salmon and mackerel, had less heart disease. He noted that Eskimos, though they ate a fairly high fat diet, had practically no heart disease. It was assumed that the fatty acids in their marine diet had made a difference in their resistance to heart disease. Because of this research, I began to take some pills high in Omega 3 fatty acids. Both the diet and schedule changes enabled me to continue coaching without further coronary episodes.

During the spring of 1994, I entered a heart disease prevention program sponsored by Mutual of Omaha. This insurance company was investigating the possibility of reducing some of the more expensive medical interventions in heart disease. Since heart surgery is very expensive, this new program was focused on modifying a person's lifestyle, thereby eliminating the need for many surgical procedures.

Dr. Dean Ornish originated the program and witnessed a reversal in the heart disease of some of his patients because of it. This was amazing when you consider that for many years the medical community assumed that you could do little to reverse heart disease. Before Ornish published his research, most people thought you could only slow the progression of heart disease.

The Ornish program involved similar dietary changes to those I had already made, so I didn't have to modify much of my diet. However, the stress management part of his program was intriguing. He discovered that meditation and various stretching exercises were helpful in reducing stress which in turn helped reverse heart disease. He also found that support groups composed of others with heart problems had a positive effect.

I practice meditation and prayer at least twice a day for roughly 20 to 25 minutes each. This helps give me added energy and a proper focus throughout the day. The Ornish program has also given me greater flexibility as I have followed the suggested stretching exercises.

Many people raise their eyebrows when they hear about my regimen. It sounds extreme and it is. But it has given me more energy and has enabled me to stay active in a very demanding profession longer than I had thought was possible after the bypass surgery in February, 1985.

My faith has helped me handle my problem with heart disease. Once you face your own mortality, you are reminded of how brief life is. In a sense, we're all living on borrowed time. Therefore, it's important to recognize the significance of life. I had never been good at taking time to smell the roses—I'm still not real good at it. But I am getting better about taking time for things other than football. I'm still very competitive, but my experience with heart disease has hopefully taken a little of the edge off that competitive nature and enabled me to be more grateful for every day I have been given.

As we prepared for the Kansas game, I was somewhat apprehensive. The last time we had played in Lawrence was the 21-20 squeaker that we won in 1993. We had been very fortunate to win that game. Kansas' current record was 8 wins and 1 loss. They were a dangerous team with good momentum.

We flew to Kansas on November 10. We hadn't taken a plane to Kansas for many years. Everyone on the team was relieved that we didn't have to take the usual four-hour bus ride to Lawrence. For Tommie Frazier, this was much better for his swollen ankle than a lengthy bus trip would have been, as he needed to keep the ankle elevated to keep the swelling down.

However, the way we played in the first half, it seemed like we were still thinking about the plane ride. We had a slow start against a highly-motivated Kansas team. I was afraid of a possible letdown against Kansas. We had been through a difficult stretch of games. It's hard for a team to stay mentally sharp and emotionally ready week after week throughout the season. That's the reason it's nearly impossible for a team to go undefeated. I knew there would be at least one game during the season where we could be upset. It was beginning to look like the odds were catching up with us.

Kansas out-yarded us 199 to 110 in the first half, but we still had an 11-point lead at halftime. We scored twice. One score came from a fumbled punt that Jon Vedral recovered in the end zone. Then a turnover gave us good field position, resulting in a short scoring drive. Although the score was 14-3, I was uneasy because Kansas had outplayed us.

At the half, I didn't rant and rave because I knew our players were trying as hard as they could. It was simply a matter of Kansas playing better. We made a few adjustments and tried to encourage our team to play with more emotion.

The second half was almost a flip-flop of the first. We generated 265 yards of offense in the second half and scored 27 unanswered points. Although Tommie Frazier's leg was sore, he ran for 99 yards on 10 carries and scored two touchdowns. One run was unbelievable! He faked three tacklers out of their shoes on the way to the 1-yard line. Tommie's 185 yards of total offense broke Jerry Tagge's 24-year-old school record for total offense. His touchdown pass to Vershan Jackson was the 42nd of his career, which broke David Humm's record of 41.

Kansas had hurt our defense during the first half with their short passing game. Finally, we shut down their passing game in the second half. We held them to only 72 yards rushing for the entire game. Because they normally have an excellent running game, I was surprised by how few yards they gained on the ground.

The most important statistic in the game involved turnovers. Kansas lost five and we scored 27 points from those turnovers. We had three turnovers ourselves—the first turnovers we had had in five games. Tommie Frazier threw an interception and we lost two fumbles. Fortunately, Kansas' five turnovers more than offset our own mistakes.

Our final score came when Mike Fullman intercepted a pass and returned the interception 86 yards with about seven minutes remaining in the game. Ben Rutz, the Kansas quarterback who threw the interception, started his career at Nebraska the same year that Tommie came to Nebraska. Later, Ben transferred to a junior college and eventually went to the University of Kansas.

Ahman Green started the game at I-back, and he and Lawrence Phillips each carried 10 times for less than 50 yards. Both played well. Lawrence was getting some quickness back, but Tommie did most of the damage running the football.

After the game was over, Tommie left the dressing room on crutches because he aggravated the soreness in his ankle. It was a hard-fought game that was good to get behind us. The stadium was full, unusual for Kansas games. But then again, nearly half of the entire crowd of over 50,000 were dressed in red. I was pleased to see how many fans followed us to Lawrence. I know the players were amazed at how many Nebraskans were there to support them. Several remarked that it was almost like a home game.

15

THE FINAL
BIG EIGHT GAME

As the season progressed, the national rankings became more important. Early season rankings really don't mean much. Until you play a few games, there is no way to judge the talent of a team. After three or four games, relative strengths and weaknesses become more apparent. Toward the end of the season it is important to be ranked high to have a chance to play for the national championship.

After we had beaten Kansas, we were 10-0 and could sense the possibility of winning back-to-back national championships. There were two other teams also contending for the national championship—Florida and Ohio State. If Nebraska and Florida ended the season ranked No. 1 and No. 2, then we would play in the Fiesta Bowl for the national championship. Of course, that would be great for the Bowl Alliance. Under this arrangement, the Orange, Sugar and Fiesta bowls rotate the national championship game every third year. If, on the other hand, Ohio State was ranked number No. 1 or No. 2, we would not be able to play them in a national championship game as they were tied to the Rose Bowl as Big Ten Champion.

Ohio State not only had a good football team, but they also received an endorsement from Penn State's Coach, Joe Paterno. "Compare what they've done to what anybody else in the country has done, and it's hard for me to believe that anybody should be rated ahead of Ohio State." I'm sure Joe's statement may have influenced some voters, particularly in the east. We didn't have much choice but to focus on football and hope we could play well enough to end up controlling our destiny in the national championship race.

We had faced an awkward situation at the end of 1994. Penn State was undefeated and playing in the Rose Bowl while Nebraska was undefeated and playing in the Orange Bowl. In 1995, all Division I football teams, except those in the Big Ten and Pac-Ten, joined the Bowl Alliance. This agreement dissolved conference tie-ups and allowed the top-ranked teams to play each other. In '94 we wanted to play an undefeated Penn State, but were forced to play Miami because of our bowl agreement. Likewise, Penn State had no choice but to play Oregon in the Rose Bowl.

In 1995, things were different with the advent of the Bowl Alliance. I couldn't understand why the Big Ten and Pac-Ten had not joined the Bowl Alliance. It makes sense to involve all the conferences in the Alliance so we don't have to worry about a deserving team being left out of the national championship. I'm guessing tradition may be the main reason that neither the Big Ten nor Pac-Ten will give up their Rose Bowl agreement.

At one time, the larger payoff of the Rose Bowl was cited as the main reason the Big Ten and Pac-Ten wouldn't consider dropping their contracts. However, now the Bowl Alliance payoff is competitive with the Rose Bowl, so that argument no longer seems valid.

I'm often asked if I'm in favor of a college football playoff. I believe if every team would get involved with the Alliance, then we would have the equivalent of a playoff. The regular season is part of the playoff. Any team that lost a game or two, particularly if the losses occurred late in the season, would be eliminated from the national championship picture. However, it's possible to lose a game early in the season and still have a chance to play for the national championship.

I would also like to see a computerized rating system. I think there is too much subjectivity in the current rating system. Whether coaches or sportswriters do the voting, the balloting isn't always free from personal bias, regionalism or poor research. A computer ranking based on common, quantifiable standards such as win-loss record, strength of schedule and margin of victory could be the basis of the rankings.

I'm not sure it's possible to ever develop the perfect playoff system for the national championship. If you have a four-team playoff at the end of the season, the fifth-ranked team is going to be upset. If you have an eight-team playoff, the ninth-ranked team will feel slighted and so on.

Thankfully, we had an open date following the Kansas game. Tommie Frazier had a sore ankle and foot, so it's doubtful that he could have played the following week. Tommie wasn't the only injured player. Our starting tight end, Mark Gilman, and one of our defensive tackles, Jason Peter, were not at full speed. We were hoping to get Tim Carpenter, one of our top two tight ends, back for the Oklahoma game. Tim had arthroscopic surgery to remove a torn cartilage a few weeks before. He was a very good blocker and would be a welcome addition against a strong Oklahoma defensive football team.

Oklahoma was 5-4-1. I was amazed that they didn't have a better record. At the beginning of the season, I thought they might be the most difficult opponent on our schedule. They had many returning starters and had played great defense against us the year before.

Saturday, November 18, was the first break we had away from football since early August. Football is grueling during the season. You must work seven days a week without a break. While preparing for football games, you can't even set aside part of your day to relax. Once the season starts, it's non-stop football. However, since we had an open date, I took Will, my 3-year-old grandson, shopping during the morning. It was great spending time with Will, but by the afternoon I was back watching film of Oklahoma. As long as we have a game to play, I can't break free from football. Obviously, the Oklahoma game was important. I was especially concerned about their fine athletes.

As I glanced at the Sunday newspaper the next day, I noticed there was no mention of Nebraska being the Big Eight Champion. Kansas State lost to Colorado, so we were the undisputed Big Eight Champions, even if we lost to Oklahoma. The other teams in the Big Eight had at least two losses. Besides being Big Eight Champs, we had also secured a spot in the Bowl Alliance. This meant we would share at least $8 million with the other members of the Big Eight.

Many fans were so focused on the national championship that they ignored the Big Eight Championship. When we had won a Big Eight Championship in previous years, it was often seen as a major accomplishment. More recently, a conference championship has been seen as commonplace.

After giving the players the weekend off, we resumed practice the Monday before the Oklahoma game. We continued to keep our focus and practice well. I'm sure the players could feel how close we were to playing for another national championship.

On Thanksgiving, we had our Thanksgiving meal at the training table with players, coaches, coaches' families and those players' families who were in town. Many don't realize the sacrifice players and coaches make during holidays. During the past 30 years, we've usually played a game on or near Thanksgiving. This means our players don't get a chance to go home for the Thanksgiving break. We've also played in a bowl game 32 of the past 34 years, so Christmas has been disrupted as well. While most students go home for at least three weeks at Christmas time, our players normally spend less than a week at home after the bowl game. Most don't spend either Christmas or New Year's Day with their families.

Thursday night before the Oklahoma game we stayed, as we normally do, at the Nebraska Center for Continuing Education. This is a small hotel on the University of Nebraska East Campus. That evening I reminisced about the 180 games I had stayed there as a coach. It's a good place to keep a team before a game since it's very quiet. Those nights before games were always lonely and anxious times for me. There were usually so many variables to consider the next day. But I would always come to the same conclusion—there are just some things a coach can't control.

On this evening, one of our linebackers, Terrell Farley, arrived at the hotel about 45 minutes after the rest of the team returned from a movie. Terrell had fallen asleep during the movie. No one noticed him sleeping, so he awoke about a half hour after the team left the theater. Of course, he was really embarrassed. This was the first time I could remember a player being late because he fell asleep during the movie. The one thing you expect in coaching is the unexpected. Whenever you work with young people, you had better be ready to be surprised. About the time you think you have seen it all, something comes out of the blue that dumbfounds you.

We played Oklahoma the day after Thanksgiving so we could accommodate a national television audience. The final home game of the season is traditionally an emotional time for players and coaches. Our seniors are introduced individually to the crowd before the game begins. This class of 21 seniors had an amazing string of victories. They had won 34 games and lost only one during the previous three seasons. Several of them had been on our campus for the past five years and won five straight Big Eight Championships.

I can't think of any group of players I haven't enjoyed working with during my coaching career. When we recruited this particular class, they were considered by most analysts to be just an average recruiting class. But this group was important to me because of their strong desire and tenacity to win. This class also showed a great deal of unity and concern for one another.

As our players were introduced before the Oklahoma game, I shook hands with each of them. I had to reflect on how unique each player was.

Reggie Baul started his athletic career as a soccer player, switched to football and improved each year at Nebraska. He became a real threat as a receiver and worked hard to improve his blocking.

Tyrone Williams was a very gifted athlete who grew up in a tough section of Palmetto, Florida, and was raised by his grandmother. He made great strides in his personal and academic life after coming to Nebraska. He turned into a great cornerback.

Tony Veland was recruited as a quarterback, but after suffering a broken collarbone and a torn patellar tendon earlier in his career, switched to safety. Tony's intellect and character paid off. He became a key player for us during his final two years. He was an excellent team captain in his own soft-spoken way.

Tommie Frazier was the most competitive athlete I have ever coached. He played better and sooner than any freshman I had been around. Then he continued to get better each year. He was a key factor in our winning back-to-back national championships.

Brook Berringer had many admirable personal qualities. He was able to handle playing behind Tommie Frazier much of his career. Few players with Brook's talent could have kept their ego from getting the best of them in this situation. Without Brook's leadership, we couldn't have won the first of our back-to-back championships. Not only was he a great athlete, but he loved the outdoors more than anyone I had coached.

Jeff Makovicka was a walk-on player from an eight-man football team. We moved him from I-back to fullback. He transformed himself in the weight room into an outstanding player who contributed to our national championships. He also made great progress as a blocker.

Clinton Childs had enough talent and ability to play either I-back or fullback. He came from a tough neighborhood in Omaha. At Nebraska I witnessed a good deal of personal growth in Clinton. He had a great game earlier in the season against Arizona State, but then suffered a very disappointing injury. Clinton was a very physical, and versatile player who helped us in many ways.

Jacques Allen spent much of his football career at Nebraska on the scout team, but he always maintained a great attitude, a sense of humor, and, above all, gave 100 percent in every practice. If ever a scout team player made a great contribution to a football team, it was Jacques Allen. He also liked to tease me whenever possible. He especially enjoyed using the bus driver's microphone on our bus rides to and from the practice field in Phoenix. His running commentary, mostly about me, gave me a headache, but Jacques and his friends got a kick out of it.

Clester Johnson came to us as a fine high school quarterback and made the transition to wingback. He became a great blocker and an excellent receiver. His steady progress made him an invaluable part of our football team. Because of Clester's personality, he was great for our team chemistry. You could always count on him for a big smile.

Darren Schmadeke was another walk-on player who played as a backup. He never missed a workout and gave us depth at the cornerback position. I always appreciated his attitude and the contribution he made to our team.

Phil Ellis was relatively small for a middle linebacker, but had excellent football instincts. Somehow he always knew where the ball was. He improved throughout his career and became a great football player in his junior and senior years. He was also an excellent team leader and captain. Phil was one of those players you could count on to give you everything he had on every play.

Doug Colman was a heavily recruited player out of New Jersey. He underwent some early disappointments in his career, but steadily improved. His size, strength, and ability to play the run made him a great player as he teamed with Phil Ellis at the middle linebacker spot. Though Doug didn't say much, he was very intense. I watched him grow personally and spiritually during his years at Nebraska.

Aaron Penland was a walk-on player who never started for us and played sparingly as a linebacker. His main asset was physical toughness, which he used to great advantage on the kicking teams. He did a tremendous job covering punts and kickoffs, which is an important phase of the game. Aaron is a very committed Christian whose spiritual leadership and character were important to the team.

Aaron Graham was a great center whose versatility was his strong suit. He could deep-snap, he could pass-block, he could run-block and he was a great leader and team captain. He was both an All-American and an Academic All-American. He also won the top NCAA academic award, the Top Eight Award. He led by example and had the respect of everyone.

Christian Peter was an intense competitor who loved physical contact. He had an unusual sense of humor that kept everyone loose. As a captain, he served as a fine leader who kept our defense motivated. Christian was also the main spokesman when the captains addressed the team just prior to taking the field.

Luther Hardin was recruited as a defensive lineman. Early in his career he lost weight and was moved to rush end where he made steady improvement. Although never a starter, Luther was a major contributor during his final two years. He became an excellent student and plans to go on to graduate school.

Brian Nunns was a special player to me because of his commitment to our program. He worked as hard as any player on the team. Though he didn't play much, he made enough progress to go from a very marginal walk-on to a solid reserve offensive lineman who was a great asset. I never doubted Brian's loyalty or commitment.

Steve Volin was another walk-on player who, through diligence and hard work, transformed himself into a very capable offensive lineman. Steve was gifted academically and will attend medical school. He is another player who will make a significant contribution to society because of his intelligence and character.

Steve Ott was a 210-pound offensive lineman from Henderson, Nebraska. Through diligence in the weight room he got bigger and became an excellent player. He suffered a major injury at Kansas State in his junior season when he broke his leg. He recovered from his injury to have a great senior year and was a major force in our offensive line.

Mark Gilman was a great all-around athlete from Montana. Mark, like many of our seniors, worked hard in the weight room. He was named Lifter of the Year. He had good hands and could always be counted on for clutch receptions.

Jason Jenkins was the lone junior college player among the seniors. He still managed to graduate in four years and was an excellent pass rusher. His playing time was limited to backup status, but he was a great team player. I also admired and appreciated his strong spiritual commitment and character.

This group of seniors illustrates how a team of athletes can accomplish much more than the separate members working individually. That's what many coaches call "synergy." The whole was truly greater than the sum of its parts. There was excellent individual talent, but it was their ability to pull together as a team that helped them perform at the highest level possible. I was proud to be their coach.

We played the final Big Eight football game on a nice afternoon, considering it was November 24. The temperature was 45 degrees, and there was a stiff wind out of the south. Oklahoma entered the game with five wins, four losses and a tie. However, they had enough talent to easily have been undefeated going into our game. Although their season had been disappointing, our game gave them a chance to redeem themselves. They also had two weeks to prepare for our game, so I wasn't sure if we could beat them the way many thought we would.

Oklahoma had two excellent running backs in James Allen and Gerald Moore. They also had an excellent tight end, Steven Alexander, and a great defensive front seven. If there was a difference in talent between our teams, it was at quarterback. I felt we definitely had an edge with Brook and Tommie.

Because of the strong wind behind them, Oklahoma kicked the ball out of the end zone. Then we began a drive that ended with a 31-yard field goal by Kris Brown. On the next series, Jamel Williams intercepted an Oklahoma pass at the Oklahoma 36-yard line and returned it for a touchdown. The ensuing extra point put us ahead 10-0. We were only midway through the first quarter, so the game was far from over. I thought by jumping out to an early lead that Oklahoma might lose their confidence.

Oklahoma changed quarterbacks in the second quarter, going with Garrick McGee. He promptly threw an interception that was returned by Michael Booker to the Oklahoma 44. Then on the next drive we missed a field-goal attempt, but we still held the lead 10-0. Before halftime we put together another drive and Kris Brown kicked a 27-yard field goal with one second remaining on the clock. At the half, we were ahead 13-0.

The game went about the way I thought it would. Both defenses played very well. While Oklahoma couldn't move the football on us, our offense struggled more than usual against their defense. In the middle of the third quarter, we got a big play from our defense that probably clinched the victory for us. Jared Tomich and Terrell Farley stripped the football from the Oklahoma tailback. Tony Veland scooped up the ball and ran for a 57-yard touchdown. Now I was more confident of the outcome. I didn't think our defense would let us down with our 20-0 lead. Not long after Tony's fumble return, Mike Fullman had a fine 48-yard punt return to the Oklahoma 32. However, we couldn't capitalize on the good field position and eventually settled for another field goal from Kris Brown. Early in the fourth quarter, Tommie Frazier hit Jon Vedral for a 38-yard touchdown. Our lead was now 30-0, so there wasn't much doubt about who would win. The touchdown pass capped the finest offensive drive of the day that consisted of five plays and 74 yards. Our final touchdown was scored by our No. 3 fullback Joel Makovicka. With less than a minute left, Joel ran off the right side of our line and broke two tackles to make the final score 37-0.

Although Tommie played well, I knew he didn't have the numbers against Oklahoma to impress many Heisman Trophy voters. It wasn't possible for us to push Oklahoma's defense up and down the field like we had against so many other teams. We still managed 407 yards of total offense while holding Oklahoma to only 241 total yards. We beat them in nearly every phase of the game.

The Oklahoma series has turned around for us in recent years. We had many disappointing losses to Oklahoma in the 1970s. But we put together an excellent record against Oklahoma in the latter part of the '80s and throughout the '90s. In the minds of most Nebraska fans, coaches, and players, the Nebraska-Oklahoma rivalry will always epitomize Big Eight football at its very best. I was sorry to see the Big Eight end and for the yearly Nebraska-Oklahoma rivalry to end as well. With the Big Twelve schedule, we'll only play them half the time.

The Oklahoma win gave us our third straight undefeated regular season. It also capped a season that resulted in some offensive records. We averaged 556 yards per game and over 52 points a game, Nebraska season records. Our rushing game was particularly outstanding in that we averaged seven yards per carry. Tommie Frazier, Aaron Graham and Jared Tomich were named first-team All-Americans. We also had 11 players named to All-Big Eight teams, seven players named to the Academic All-Big Eight team, and Aaron Graham became our 56th Academic All-American in football. It had been a great year, yet our locker room after the game was relatively calm. Clearly, we hadn't reached our goal. Most people in Nebraska, including our players, expected us to win the national championship. We were now in position to do just that. We would soon begin preparing for the Fiesta Bowl and our third straight national championship game.

16

A Very Long 48 Hours

We have many Nebraskans who live in Arizona and California, and they, along with thousands of Nebraskans, created tremendous pressure for Fiesta Bowl tickets. We had 45,000 ticket orders from members of booster clubs alone. Therefore, the average fan who hadn't made a contribution to the athletic department didn't have much of a chance to get tickets. Many fans who donated to our athletic department were disappointed when they, too, discovered there just weren't enough tickets for everyone. Unfortunately, only the major donors were guaranteed Fiesta Bowl tickets.

Our players felt the ticket crunch as well. They were inundated with requests from family and friends. Each player was limited to four tickets in accordance with NCAA rules. We asked the players who would not be playing to offer their tickets to their teammates if possible. It was permissible for one player to give his four tickets to another if he didn't need them. Unfortunately, almost everyone right down to the scout team players had people whom they knew who were going to the game. I was concerned that the ticket shortage might distract our players. I knew many seniors were anxious about getting tickets for their immediate families.

Financially, college football has made quite a change since I started coaching. When I began coaching in the early 1960s, part of the athletic scholarship was $15 a month for "laundry" money. When you adjust this figure for inflation, the $15 a month would probably exceed $70 per month today. In the 1960s, players were also given free passes to most of the movie theaters in Lincoln. They received travel jackets that they could wear when we were on the road and occasionally wore them to social events. It was not uncommon for players to sell their complimentary tickets to fans. This was something we didn't encourage, but it was a common practice throughout college football. Today's college football player would be penalized severely if he sold his tickets to anyone, received incidental expense money or free movie passes. Generally, a football player today receives fewer benefits than his predecessor of 30 years ago.

The entire budget of the University of Nebraska Athletic Department for the 1960-1961 fiscal year was $875,000. Football brought in $748,000. In 1994-1995 the total budget was $25.725 million. Expenses for football in 1994-95 were $9.3 million and the football income was $21.9 million, a net gain of $12.6 million.

Football has been asked to become more and more profitable. In recent years, our coaching staff has been reduced by three graduate assistant coaches and one on-campus recruiting coordinator. Football scholarships were cut from 95 to 85. We went from the entire squad being included in early fall practice to a limit of

105. Our paid recruiting visits to our campus were reduced from 85 to 56, and the time allowed to make recruiting visits to prospects was cut back dramatically. So, in many ways, we have been asked to produce more revenue with fewer resources.

Title IX, the government regulation intended to promote gender equity in our nation's schools, has affected football in recent years and may affect it even more in the future. Unfortunately, for male athletes, proportionality has been the primary measure of compliance with Title IX. If 60 percent of a student population is female and 40 percent is male, then a strictly proportional interpretation would mean that female athletes should receive 60 percent of a school's athletic scholarships and men would receive 40 percent. Football is the great imbalancer at many schools as women don't have a corresponding sport with a squad size as large as football.

Football coaches favor increased opportunities for women. Women's sports generally fare much better at schools with major income-producing men's football and basketball programs. It takes a great deal of money to support a full complement of men's and women's sports. There are some women's groups who promote proportionality at the expense of pre-existing men's sports. Men's wrestling, swimming and gymnastics programs are disappearing at an alarming rate. Some schools have dropped football entirely to accommodate Title IX. The decrease in football scholarships from 95 to 85 in recent years was prompted to some degree by Title IX. There are special interest groups now advocating cutbacks in football scholarships to as few as 60.

I believe that many of the original objectives of Title IX were laudable. In recent years, the implementation of this regulation has gone the way of many government programs. It has been interpreted in ways that have taken it far from what it was originally intended to do.

Football players realize that they receive little of the income they generate. Many live near the poverty level, yet they help produce more than $20 million in revenue for our program. More than half of the Division I athletic departments around the country are either losing money or breaking even. Of course, if these programs were to pay athletes, it would be a terrible strain on their budgets. The excess money generated by football and men's basketball is being spent on non-revenue sports, on facilities and administration.

I know it's frustrating for some players to see the university administrative party, which includes administrators, coaches, faculty and their families attend the bowl games at athletic department expense. Often the players' families have a difficult time affording the bowl trip. Sometimes family members can't find enough tickets except from scalpers.

The NCAA should consider doing more financially to help student-athletes. I doubt that the NCAA would approve a stipend. Possibly, they would consider providing two or three expense-paid round trips home for an athlete each year. Another proposal that makes sense to me is to allow an athlete to sell his unused complimentary tickets back to the athletic department. In football, four tickets sold back at an average price of $25 would generate $100 a game. Therefore, a player could receive more than $1,000 a year for unused tickets, assuming his parents or others didn't need them. In most cases, the athletic department could sell the returned tickets so there wouldn't be a net loss of revenue.

It's easy to see why many athletes are targets for dishonest agents and runners. For financial reasons, athletes are tempted to enter the NFL draft early. Our players aren't allowed to earn income during the school year. Even during the summer months, it's not easy to earn money because they often use much of their time to prepare for the upcoming season and attend summer school. The athlete is in a bind. He receives less financially, is under more pressure to perform academically and athletically and also receives more scrutiny from the media.

Not long after the Oklahoma game, the TV program "48 Hours" did a program on violent athletes. As we expected, our football program and the Lawrence Phillips assault were featured. Many statements made during the broadcast were either inaccurate or misleading.

During the program, Sandy Worm, a resident of the apartment building where the Lawrence Phillips assault occurred, said, "I saw Lawrence Phillips at the time of his assault pounding the victim's head against the wall." Jim Griesen, Vice Chancellor for Student Affairs and Linda Schwartzkopf, Director of Student Judicial Affairs, interviewed Ms. Worm as a part of their investigation into the incident. In the course of that interview, it became clear that she only saw Lawrence holding her head against the wall with his hands, and did not see any movement to or from the wall. After interviewing four eyewitnesses, Jim and Linda concluded that Lawrence was not "pounding the victim's head against the wall." The program also implied that the victim's head was hit against the mailboxes at the apartment—which was false.

Jeff Benedict appeared on the show as an expert on sports violence. When Benedict had phoned me several weeks before the program was aired, he said he was with "The Center for the Study of Sports in Society." When he began to ask me questions, he said they would be related to "research" on violence in athletics. As I listened to his questions, they seemed more like questions a reporter would ask than a researcher, so I ended the interview. I wasn't surprised when he appeared on the "48 Hours" program.

Richard Lapchick, the Director of "The Center for the Study of Sports in Society," disagrees with the "research" cited by Benedict. Lapchick said Benedict's conclusions were based on a study including a small sample of only 65 cases and did not control for key factors such as alcohol use.

Lapchick cites some interesting statistics. According to him, in 1995 three million women were battered, 72 by college and professional athletes. Of 50,000 college football players, there were 38 cases of assault. These figures hardly bear out the commonly held thesis that athletes are more violent than others in our society. Many of the charges against Nebraska football players featured prominently on "48 Hours" would not have made the fine print of the local newspaper had they not involved athletes. Heightened visibility is both a wonderful and terrible thing.

I was disappointed that "48 Hours" included statements by Melissa DeMuth. DeMuth was a topless dancer who claimed that Christian Peter had allegedly assaulted her a few years ago. The case was investigated by the police, her claims were not substantiated and no charges were filed.

Unlike the report by Bernard Goldberg on CBS Evening News, the "48 Hours" people did talk to me and tried to get me to interview for their program. I had heard that they were including Kathy Redmond and some of her allegations concerning

Christian Peter on their show. I knew Kathy and was familiar with her charges.

I told the people representing "48 Hours" that her charges were four and a half years old and that they had been investigated by University of Nebraska police, Lincoln police and the County Attorney's office. The allegations were unsubstantiated and no charges were ever filed. I thought that it was wrong to present information that authorities had found to be of no substance on a national television program. If these types of charges were to be allowed, someone could say almost anything about another person with apparent impunity.

I told "48 Hours" that if they were going to include Kathy and her allegations on their program, they could count me out. I did not want to be on a program of the type that seemed to be taking shape.

Some have thought that my failure to be on the program was a mistake, that I should have rebutted some of the claims made. There was no way that I could control what comments of mine the producers would include and what they would edit out, or even what footage they might show over my voice. It did not seem wise to lend credibility to their show by appearing on it.

Shelley Smith, who is a reporter for *Sports Illustrated,* stated on the "48 Hours" program that in the Lawrence Phillips case I had been at the victim's house Monday after the assault and visited with her family. The victim's family's home is more than 150 miles from Lincoln. Obviously, this too was not true. The family of the victim later told me that when they were contacted by "48 Hours," they informed "48 Hours" that I did not drive to their home. Although "48 Hours" knew I hadn't gone to the victim's home, they still reported that I did. As stated previously, I visited with the parents and the victim in the UNL women's basketball office, at the request of the women's basketball coach.

Erin Moriarty, a correspondent on the show, while talking to Jason Jenkins' attorney, said that Jason's victim was "paid off." She implied that Jeremy Sperling was paid to not press charges against him. Jason Jenkins was a lineman who hit Sperling in the head with a bottle, which caused him to lose sight in one eye.

Clearly, the facts show that Sperling was not paid off. According to Hal Anderson, who represented Jason Jenkins, Sperling and his family had their attorney contact Hal to propose a settlement outside of court. The prosecutor accepted the civil settlement reached by the attorneys for Jason and Sperling. The settlement was a $24,000 payment from Jason to Sperling. Sperling recommended to the prosecution, as part of the settlement, that the charges against Jason be reduced from a felony to a misdemeanor. Sperling would receive additional money if Jason made an NFL team.

Jason's account of the incident and Jeremy Sperling's were quite different. Jeremy claimed he was tripped or pushed into Jason and that Jason hit him in the eye with the bottle. Jason claimed Jeremy Sperling threw a punch at him, and, as he ducked, the bottle he was holding came up reflexively and hit Sperling. Jason claimed the injury was an accident. Jason's brother paid $24,000 to Sperling at the Sperlings' request. Everyone hoped the money would pay for a surgery to restore Jeremy's eyesight. Jeremy was not "paid off" as stated in the program. He simply got what he and his family requested from Jason.

For me, the most disturbing part of the "48 Hours" report was a statement from an anonymous person who was supposedly a member of the Lincoln criminal justice system. I've always felt it's unethical and cowardly to use anonymous sources when making accusations. An anonymous source can say anything without being accountable for his or her remarks. This shadowy figure said, "We have to humbly present ourselves to the coaching staff in order to seek an audience with a football player." It was also said that football players are treated like the governor of the state "only more respectful." This type of rhetoric is pure hogwash. I have coached at Nebraska for more than 30 years and I've never known a law enforcement official who had to humbly present himself to the football staff so they could talk to a member of the team. Our dialogue with the Lincoln Police and the Campus Police has always been straightforward. And the more direct everyone is, the better.

The same anonymous source said an assistant football coach took a gun he obtained from Tyrone Williams and kept it locked in a desk drawer for two days, though we were aware that the Lincoln Police were searching for it. This allegation really bothered me. Erin Moriarty, a correspondent from "48 Hours," had called and asked me about this event. I referred her to Ken Cauble, the Campus Chief of Police. Cauble said he discussed the incident with her for nearly an hour. He told her that Kevin Steele, the assistant coach, informed him about the weapon. Cauble told her that Kevin Steele followed his instructions by locking it in the desk drawer, and that there was absolutely no attempt by anyone in the football office to conceal the weapon. To have disregarded Chief Cauble's statement seemed irresponsible. After talking with me and Cauble, "48 Hours" knew what the facts were. The facts apparently didn't make much of a story.

Moriarty also asked me on the telephone if I had compared a .22-caliber revolver to a BB gun. I told her I had never said this. I know the difference between a .22-caliber weapon and a BB gun. I informed her twice that this statement was erroneous. Still "48 Hours" ran the piece making it sound as though I was either minimizing the power of a .22-caliber revolver or was just plain stupid. I have compared a .22-caliber weapon to a pellet gun because the two weapons do have about the same penetrating power. Maybe someone heard me say something like this and confused a pellet gun with a BB gun.

Obviously, the "48 Hours" program damaged our football program's reputation. Moriarty told me she would call me after the program aired to discuss it with me. I'm still waiting for her call.

I am very sorry that several of our players have been in trouble with the law. However, "48 Hours" left the impression that these problems were all recent and went unpunished. Jason Jenkins' incident was in April of 1993, more than two and a half years before the "48 Hours" program was aired. I suspended Jason from the team for a period of time. He has followed through on the requirements of the courts. He graduated in four years and has had no trouble with the law since the episode with Sperling.

Christian Peter first came to my attention in 1991. Frank Solich, our backfield coach, brought a film of a high school scrimmage to me and asked me to look at a defensive lineman named Christian Peter. I looked at the film and was very impressed with Christian's strength and effort. This was the only film available of Christian's senior season as he was ruled ineligible to play shortly after the scrimmage. New Jersey officials ruled that he had exhausted his high school eligibility after attending three different high schools. We normally would not offer a scholarship to a young man with only a scrimmage film to go on; however, Christian was so impressive on that one film that we decided to recruit him. Very few people knew much about him because he didn't play in his senior year so it came down to Christian's choosing Nebraska over Temple, our only other competitor.

We thought that Christian had met NCAA academic requirements for a scholarship. However, in August of 1991, after Christian was already on our campus, our admissions staff decided that one of his high school credits was in doubt so he was ineligible to play. Since he didn't play in his senior year of high school or his first year of college, he was understandably rusty when he returned to the field in his second year of college and ended up redshirting.

During his redshirt year, Christian was charged with urinating in public and minor in possession of alcohol, which I didn't know about, was charged with verbally threatening a parking attendant who was towing his car, and finally, was charged with third-degree sexual assault for allegedly grabbing a young woman, Natalie Kuijvenhoven, in the crotch in a Lincoln bar.

The sexual assault charge was filed in May of 1993, two and a half years before the "48 Hours" program ran. At the time, Christian had been a reserve lineman and his ability to play for us was still very much in doubt. Christian was charged with a misdemeanor, so he was required to pay a fine and do community service work. I suspended him from the football team for a time. I also told him that his suspension would be permanent if there was more trouble of any kind. He was required to stay out of bars, quit using alcohol and to enter an alcohol treatment program. He faithfully followed this program over the next three years. He also did satisfactorily in school and continued to perform well on the field. I felt he had matured in his personal life. At no time did Christian ever test positive for steroids or street drugs, and he was tested randomly several times a year.

Unfortunately, the incident where Christian pled no contest to grabbing Natalie Kuijvenhoven was far from over. Nearly three years later, it came back to haunt him. Natalie appeared on television describing the incident. Then Christian became the target of several special interest groups fighting abusive behavior.

Christian denied grabbing Natalie even when first charged in 1993. He eventually decided to plead no contest to the charge rather than endure a trial over a matter that was a misdemeanor offense. Looking back on it, he now regrets that decision.

Christian thought that even if he was blamed for the incident that the charge would be minor and would eventually be forgotten. Natalie was a former Miss Nebraska and a television reporter, and it never did go away.

In March of 1996, Christian pled no contest to disturbing the peace in Kearney, Nebraska. Before this incident he had stayed away from alcohol for nearly three years and kept out of trouble. Christian was active in community service, was generous with his time in children's activities and was an outstanding team leader. He received more votes than anyone on our team when we elected captains for the 1995 football team. He was almost certain to be a solid draft pick in the upcoming NFL draft.

The incident in Kearney suddenly seemed to negate everything Christian had done in the previous three years. According to Christian and Brian Nunns, another player with Christian, Janelle Mues called Christian a rapist. Christian admits to having responded with a good deal of profanity. He denies putting his hand on her throat and shoving her as she claims. It seemed strange that no one in the crowded bar saw Christian push Mues. Authorities could find no one who witnessed Christian push or grab her. They found no witnesses to substantiate a report by an anonymous person referred to in *Sports Illustrated* as saying Christian "grabbed the backsides of women" in the bar. Christian had been drinking after three years of abstinence, used bad language, bad judgment and was suddenly perceived again as a public menace. Christian had left his alcohol counseling program after the 1995 season, apparently thinking he could handle alcohol without help. Christian is not an alcoholic but is one of those people who doesn't behave well when he drinks. He was to pay a great price for his mistake.

Christian left school shortly after the Kearney incident out of embarrassment and frustration. I hope he will eventually return to finish his college degree. Christian has caused some of his own problems, but not nearly to the extent reported by the press. Few players have suffered from as much negative publicity as Christian. Some of it has not been accurate.

The incident involving Tyrone Williams, in which he was alleged to have fired a .22-caliber revolver at a moving car, has been tied up in court for more than two years. The County Attorney's office charged him with two felonies. But the Public Defender's office maintained that the two charges were nearly identical, so Tyrone was being subjected to double jeopardy.

Tyrone's case was turned over to the Public Defender's office.

I suspended Tyrone for the spring game and the first game of the season in 1994. He was suspended for using alcohol the night of the incident and for possessing a handgun. I couldn't pass judgment on whether he was guilty of the charges against him. That was something that needed to be resolved in court.

Dennis Keefe, the Lancaster County Public Defender, presented approximately 50 cases to the County Attorney in which events were very similar to Tyrone's case. In these cases, the charges were usually reduced to misdemeanor or fourth class felonies which sometimes resulted in sentences involving probation. Most of those accused had prior criminal records where Tyrone does not. The County Attorney rejected Dennis' appeal to reduce the charges, so Tyrone remains charged with two felonies and will be tried nearly two and a half years after the incident for which he was charged. Dennis maintains that in his estimation Tyrone is being treated more harshly than others he has dealt with who had similar charges against them.

Despite being accused of interfering with the criminal justice system, I have little background that would qualify me to pass judgment on Tyrone's case in light of the 50-odd cases presented to the County Attorney by Dennis. I must admit, however, to being thoroughly confused as to why Tyrone was charged with two felonies when the person who shot Brendan Holbein and was identified by Eric Alford was never prosecuted. Also, the individual who shot Chris Norris from behind and, according to Chris, fired several other shots into his apartment was only charged with misdemeanors.

Tyrone was evaluated for alcohol abuse and was told to avoid further trouble or be permanently dismissed. He entered counseling for alcohol abuse at that time and has had no further alcohol related problems. He had no record of criminal activity before or after this incident. Tyrone is very close to graduating in four years. Considering that he has had little family support, I think he has made excellent progress both personally and academically.

Reggie Baul was charged with theft in December of 1994. He was accused of stealing a billfold. His case presented a unique problem since Reggie's charges were filed only a short time before we were to leave for the bowl game in Miami. I needed to decide if he should be allowed to play in the bowl game. However, the legal process wouldn't run its course until well after the bowl game was played. I told Reggie that he could either be suspended for the bowl game or take a polygraph test, which would indicate if he was being truthful about the incident. Reggie said he didn't take the billfold, and his father agreed to pay for the polygraph.

Reggie was given a polygraph by a licensed investigator on December 20, 1994. Here is how Reggie answered questions. "Did you take Teri's billfold off of the table at the Village Inn?" Answer no. "Did you carry Teri's billfold into the men's room at Village Inn?" Answer no. "Did you remove any property from Teri's billfold while in the men's room at Village Inn?" Answer no. "Were you ever handed Teri's property by a friend?" Answer yes. "Were you holding Teri's property for a friend?" Answer yes. "Have you specifically lied to any question I have asked you during this examination?" Answer no. The polygraph indicated that Reggie was telling the truth.

Later a young man who had been at the restaurant with Reggie admitted he took the billfold, had removed the contents from it, and had given Reggie a card from the billfold when he realized that he was about to be searched. Reggie may have been wrong for not refusing the card, but he claims he didn't know what he was being handed. After the bowl game, the charges were changed from theft to receiving stolen property. Since Reggie had the card on his person, he entered a plea of no contest to a misdemeanor charge of possession of stolen property. He was ordered to pay a fine for this. I didn't suspend Reggie from the football team because I believed the polygraph test was accurate, and the confession of Reggie's acquaintance was also truthful.

The matters concerning Riley Washington, who was charged in August of 1995, and Lawrence Phillips, who was charged in September of 1995, have already been well documented.

When you examine the criminal records of our players over the past few years, here is what you will find. Six young men cited, four of them pled guilty or no contest to misdemeanor charges and two of them have charges still pending. The records of our football team were examined exhaustively over a period of at least four and a half years. When you have 150 football players and you examine every record available over a period of four and a half years, having four misdemeanor counts that have stuck is not an exceedingly high number.

Five of the six players were suspended from the team for a game or games and all have paid a price not only in the courts, but from negative publicity. We will wait and see how the two cases with charges pending are resolved. As stated previously, I don't believe Riley Washington is guilty as charged. Tyrone Williams' attorneys maintain that he has been improperly charged.

We held a press conference following the "48 Hours" segment

so we could address some of these issues. I felt our players had been damaged by much of the misinformation. Even though I tried to make sure our players side of the story was told, not much was reported by the press. Perhaps the only good that came from my effort was to let our players know that we did care about them enough to try to present their side of the story.

The "48 Hours" story on violence in sports only served to tarnish the image of our football team. My reputation had gone from being a decent coach who couldn't win the big one to a coach who would do anything to win football games—including obstructing the criminal justice system. While some probably thought I was running a detention home for football players, I knew they were wrong. Unfortunately, I wasn't sure how many people would believe me after watching "48 Hours."

John Wooden, the former UCLA basketball coach, said, "Be more concerned with your character than with your reputation, because your character is what you really are while your reputation is merely what others think you are." I believe that John's statement is true. Hopefully my character is better than what many perceive it to be. Time will tell.

17

BIG TWELVE AND OTHER MATTERS

The Big Twelve Conference presidents met to discuss issues related to the formation of the new league on December 1, 1995. One important issue on their agenda was whether non-qualifiers should be allowed to enroll at Big Twelve schools. A non-qualifier is an athlete who does not meet academic eligibility standards for an athletic scholarship.

Nebraska took a position in favor of allowing non-qualifiers to enroll at Big Twelve schools at their own expense. We thought the statistics supported our position. Our '95 NCAA graduation rate report showed an overall football graduation rate at the University of Nebraska of 73 percent, with a 78 percent black player graduation rate and 67 percent of our white players graduating. According to the College Football Association, using a different formula, our graduation rate was 85 percent. These rates were for scholarship football athletes who enrolled during the 1988-89 school year and were the highest of any Big Twelve school. The NCAA graduation rate reported in the spring of 1996 for those student-athletes entering the 1989-90 school year at the University of Nebraska was 74 percent, with a black graduation rate of 64 percent and a white graduation rate of 88 percent. Our 1996 graduation rate was the highest of any Big Twelve school for the second year in a row. Our minority graduation rate was also tops for the two years. Our football graduation rate was nearly 25 percent higher than the student body male graduation rate.

We have taken an average of slightly over two non-qualifiers a year for the past 10 years with the promise of a scholarship if they became eligible. Most of these non-qualifiers were athletes who were close to qualifying when they signed their letters of intent in February. We thought that they would qualify when we signed them, but they came up short of qualifying by the end of their senior year of high school.

Since we had a good graduation rate and had been selective in signing a small number of non-qualifiers, we hoped the Big Twelve schools would listen to our appeal to admit non-qualifiers in the Big Twelve as we had in the Big Eight. Four schools, the University of Nebraska, University of Kansas, Kansas State and Iowa State voted to allow non-qualifiers. The other eight schools voted not to allow non-qualifiers. Only four votes were needed to keep the Big Twelve from excluding non-qualifiers. Therefore, it was decided the issue would be reviewed at the spring meetings. We assumed, and I'm sure most other Big Twelve schools assumed, that non-qualifiers could be recruited in the 1995-96 school year.

When we did a self-study, we found that of the nine minority student-athletes who had been qualifiers six years ago but would be non-qualifiers under today's higher standards, seven had graduated, and two of the seven had completed masters degrees. It seemed that non-qualifiers were graduating at about the same rate at Nebraska as those who were qualifiers academically, and to exclude non-qualifiers was going to be particularly damaging for minority students.

CBS Sports was going to broadcast the Fiesta Bowl, so we had an awkward predicament. I was not happy with how we were treated by CBS's Evening News and their "48 Hours" program. When I discussed my disappointment with CBS, CBS Sports representatives told me they didn't necessarily support everything CBS News did and that they were entirely separate from CBS News and "48 Hours." Since CBS Sports wanted to do an interview with me for the bowl game, I asked them for a chance to rebut some things said about us. Dave Kenin, the president of CBS Sports, seemed willing to let me present our side of the story.

In an interview taped by CBS Sports on December 5, I tried to make the case that we weren't a win-at-all-costs football program. Since we had never received any major football sanctions from the NCAA during the past 34 years, I explained how ridiculous this theory was. Generally, schools with a "win-at-all-costs" philosophy will break NCAA rules to gain an edge over their competition.

I also defended our school by referring to our academic record. I mentioned our excellent graduation rate. We've had more football Academic All-Americans than any other school in the nation, 56 in all. We also lead the nation in Top Eight Award winners in football, eight in all. This is the top academic award presented by the NCAA. Again, I explained how these facts didn't support CBS' criticism of our football program. Any school that only cares about winning football games will usually not place an emphasis on academics.

I also discussed our team's demeanor on the football field. We've had very few cases of inappropriate conduct during a game. And we've never had a fight or major incident take place on the field. Usually, a team that places too much emphasis on winning will resort to unethical tactics to gain a competitive edge.

Later in the interview, I discussed the charges filed against our players. I mentioned that we had had only four percent of our 150 football players charged with a crime over a four and one half year period, less than 1 percent of our team charged each year.

I remarked that it might be difficult to find 150 young men of that age bracket in any endeavor, whether it is a fraternity, a military unit, a band, or whatever, who would not have as many problems with the law. I greatly appreciated the people on CBS Sports giving me an opportunity to state my views.

As we continued to prepare for the bowl game, I was generally pleased with Lawrence Phillips' attitude. He appeared more thoughtful and caring. I was sure his counseling with John Goldrich was doing some good. I did talk with Lawrence about relationships. I emphasized the importance of his realizing there are some people who will take advantage of him whenever possible. However, I wanted Lawrence to know there were many people who supported him and would not take advantage of him. Lawrence's background made it difficult for him to trust anyone. It seemed that he was making progress in this area.

Although Lawrence himself had been badly hurt by others in his past, I hope he will continue to learn how to show compassion to others. I explained to him the significance of a relationship with God. Those who are truly affected by a sense of God's love and grace are often able to love and trust others in return. I was not sure if my words meant much to him, but I hoped he understood that I cared about him as a person, not just an athlete.

I have seen many players whose lives have been radically changed because of a changed relationship with God. For example, Irving Fryar, an outstanding wingback on the 1983 football team, experienced a dramatic conversion several years ago. Today, he still plays football in the NFL, but he is also an ordained minister who shares his Christian faith across the country. When Irving left the University of Nebraska, few would have predicted that Irving's life would change so much in just a few years.

Junior Miller, an outstanding All-American tight end for us in the 1970s, had a similar type of life-changing experience after hitting rock bottom. His NFL career was over, his personal problems seemed insurmountable, and then he had a powerful conversion experience. Junior now owns his own business here in Lincoln, has several dozen employees and has a very strong commitment to his Christian faith.

Earlier in this book, I referred to my encounter with Jimmy Williams at the Minnesota Vikings camp. Irving, Junior and Jimmy were all players I worried about when they left Nebraska as seniors. Today, each of these men is making a positive impact on others. They would be the first to say it is their relationship with Jesus that has transformed their lives. There have been many other players who have shown tremendous change in their personal lives as their spiritual lives matured.

Although it was too soon to predict if Lawrence's life would be changed because of the things he had been through, I did see him approach his teammates differently. During practice, I watched Lawrence help a defensive back off the ground after he had just run him over. Earlier in his career he would not have done that. There were several other times I observed Lawrence interacting differently with his teammates. He wasn't perfect, but he was trying hard to be a team player.

Lawrence's attorney, Hal Anderson, asked the County Attorney to move Lawrence's sentencing to a different time. He wanted a time that was unannounced to the press, so Lawrence could be sentenced without the glare of publicity. The County Attorney refused his request, which Hal said was unusual since officials normally try to accommodate the accused and move their sentencing to a convenient time. This may have been done to accommodate the press; it may also have had to do with not appearing to give athletes special treatment.

I visited with the victim's mother on December 8. She wasn't thrilled with the "48 Hours" program on sports violence. She had asked "48 Hours" not to use her daughter's name or put her picture on camera. They didn't honor her request.

The victim's mother was concerned that with Lawrence losing his chance to win the Heisman Trophy he might do something foolish. She felt his disappointment could put her daughter at risk. I assured her that Lawrence had told me he had no intention of contacting her daughter and things were going well. I was sure Lawrence wouldn't turn to violence again.

We held our first recruiting weekend Friday, Saturday and Sunday, December 8, 9 and 10. Unfortunately, the weather turned bad and was very cold. We had temperatures near zero with a very strong wind, so the wind chill was below-zero. Three of the recruits were from California, so the weather was a shock to them.

December has always been a difficult month for our coaching staff. We spend many hours preparing for a bowl game, but simultaneously we have to recruit. It's hard to do justice to either activity.

In early December, our coaches were on the road contacting recruits while I stayed in the office and ran practice. We often only had one defensive coach, one offensive coach and two graduate assistants at practice. Therefore, we could only practice effectively for about 45 minutes. We thought it was important that we continue to practice after taking off a few days after the Oklahoma game. It seemed that when we took off for any length of time, our execution and timing on offense, particularly with the option game, went downhill.

I made a mistake in 1988 when I changed our routine of bowl preparation. When discussing bowl game preparation with the Florida State coaches, I found they usually would take two weeks off after their last game and then would have only eight or nine practices before their bowl game. What worked for Florida State, certainly didn't work for us. We lost seven consecutive bowl games and didn't execute well, particularly on offense.

Nobody has ever accused me of being particularly bright. However, I eventually figured out that we should return to our previous routine of bowl preparation, which we did in 1993. Therefore, we only took off a few days after the season was over. Then, for the next two weeks, we practiced three times a week. Although these practices were short, we continued to get some work on timing and execution. For all practical purposes, we really didn't stop practicing after the last game of the season. This seemed to pay off as we nearly beat Florida State in the '93 Orange Bowl. We did beat Miami the following year in the Orange Bowl. Now we were using the same approach for our upcoming game with Florida.

Tommie Frazier failed to win the Heisman Trophy on Saturday, December 9. This was a big disappointment for everyone in our program. We felt Tommie had been the best player in college football, especially if you looked at his entire career. During the four years he played for us, we lost only three games in which he started. There was no one who was more versatile or had a greater impact on his team than Tommie. However, if you compared his statistics for just one season against other candidates, he might not win the Heisman.

Eddie George, the outstanding tailback from Ohio State, was named the winner of the Heisman Trophy. Tailbacks usually win the Heisman and Eddie had an excellent senior season.

Tommie was very gracious and handled the press well. However, I knew he was so competitive that he must have been boiling inside. But as always, Tommie showed a lot of class by refusing to complain about not receiving the Heisman Trophy. I knew, however, Tommie had something to prove against Florida. His not winning the Heisman was not good news for our opponent on January 2.

Tommie did win the Johnny Unitas Award for the outstanding college quarterback and was named to many All-American teams, so he certainly was recognized for his efforts. It's amazing that he won so many awards as an option quarterback. Most of his value to our team didn't show up on paper—unless you look at the win-loss column.

On Tuesday, December, 12, Nancy and I attended the NFL Hall of Fame dinner in New York. That morning there was a press conference at CBS, followed by a luncheon also hosted by CBS. Most of the top people at CBS Sports were there. It was a little awkward because they knew I was upset by their network's coverage of our football team. For the most part, the luncheon was amicable, however. CBS Sports was excited about broadcasting the Fiesta Bowl and was anticipating high ratings from the game.

I was presented the Distinguished American Award at the Hall of Fame Banquet that evening. Most of the previous recipients were well-known people who had distinguished themselves in government and public service. The only other coach who had received the award was Penn State's Joe Paterno.

I felt uncomfortable accepting the award for two reasons. First, I wasn't sure I deserved to be part of the select group of past award recipients. Second, I was uncomfortable about the negative publicity that Nebraska and I had received throughout the year. I had written the selection committee and asked them to reconsider presenting the award to me. Because of the negative publicity, I thought it might be better for college football and the Hall of Fame for me not to get the award. A representative of the committee responded by assuring me they still wanted to present the award to me.

After I received the award, I shared a few brief remarks with the audience. Primarily, I talked about the problems young people face today. I discussed a program Nancy and I have been involved with that helps provide a solution to these problems. We have been sponsoring young people through the Teammates program for four years. In initiating Teammates, a group of "at risk" students was selected by the counselors in the Lincoln Public Schools. Twenty-five young men were chosen from junior high school. It was doubtful that many of these students would finish high school, much less college. Each of these young men was given a mentor. Most mentors were members of our football team. We helped raise money so these young people could be given tutoring and transportation. Some were sent to summer camps, and, most importantly, we guaranteed their post-secondary education would be paid if they graduated from high school.

Last spring we were gratified to see seven of the nine high school seniors graduate from high school. All seven of those who graduated went on to college. We hope to have similar success with two more classes of Teammates. I reminded the crowd in New York that it doesn't take a huge investment of time and energy in the lives of young people to see dramatic changes.

I didn't mention Lawrence Phillips by name, but I figured the audience got my point. Unless people are willing to invest in young people and give them a chance, many of them will become liabilities to society rather than assets.

Rich Glover was inducted into the College Football Hall of Fame at the same banquet. Johnny Rodgers also attended with his new bride. Johnny was married in the Heisman room at the Downtown Athletic Club the day before. I really enjoyed seeing them at the banquet. It reminded me that we had all been together when Johnny received the Heisman Trophy in December of 1972. Simultaneously, Rich was in New York after receiving the 1972 Lombardi Award. I thought it was interesting that things had come full circle.

On December 16, we had football practice and were the host to 24 recruits and six sets of parents. This made for an extremely hectic weekend. There were two recruits who ate breakfast and then returned to their rooms to sleep. They missed their appointments with faculty members, tour of the facilities, meetings with coaches, trainers and equipment men. Of course, we lost our interest in recruiting them. As the recruits left on Sunday, I was surprised when the two late-sleeping recruits told me they had a great visit. I'm not sure what they did with their time, but it surely didn't have much to do with our football program.

Our best insight into a player's character is often provided during his weekend campus visit. Some are mostly interested in social life, some are interested in football only and some have a balanced approach to academics and football. While most recruits are respectful, some appear to lack respect for authority. It's obvious these recruits lack a set of basic values. Often the host-player is the best judge of the recruit's character. It's remarkable how much they learn in just a few short hours about a recruit. Obviously, our coaches are interested when the host-player discusses his time with the recruit.

When we recruit an athlete, we know there are two factors that have great influence on his decision to attend Nebraska when he visits our campus. We have little or no control over these factors. First, the weather or climate of Nebraska can sway an athlete away from us. When a recruit from a warm climate visits on a cold day, we make sure they understand it doesn't stay cold throughout the year in Nebraska. This past January we had a family from California land in Lincoln during a blizzard. The mother was sure they were all going to die as the plane made its approach in a blinding snowstorm. They had never been in a snowstorm before, and I doubt they will be in the future. We were certain this family was very interested in Nebraska and that the son would commit to us, but he went elsewhere. We had another recruit and his family, also from California, who initially didn't seem as interested in our program, but while visiting during the same weekend decided to come to Nebraska.

Second, the chemistry between a recruit and his host-player is another critical factor that is hard to control. No matter how hard we try to pair a host and a recruit based on their common interests, occasionally, they don't match up very well. We lost a well-known recruit recently because of an argument between the host and the recruit over a dominoes game. While our player won the dominoes game, we lost the recruit.

On Sunday, December 17, the lead story on the front page of a local paper was about the beating our football team was taking from the national press. The article was a compilation of past quotes from many sources around the country criticizing our program, and me, for playing Lawrence Phillips. The article contained releases dating back over the previous three months. My good friend, and former chancellor at the University of Nebraska, Woody Varner, called to congratulate me on receiving the Distinguished American Award. He commented that he hadn't seen anything about it in the newspaper. He was concerned about the negativism and lack of publicity on something positive. I told Woody something that he already knew, negative stories receive more coverage than positive ones.

When visiting with recruits around the country, I found the negative publicity about our program didn't hinder recruiting as much as I first thought it would. One recruit's father in Florida told me he was pleased I gave Lawrence Phillips a second chance. Many parents were glad I hadn't cast Lawrence aside once he appeared to be more of a liability than an asset to our football program. I'm sure they hoped I would support their son if he also needed help.

Most parents realize that it's possible for their son to make a mistake that could ruin his life. For me, it was a relief to know that someone appreciated my efforts to help a player in trouble. I was convinced we were doing the right thing. I was hopeful our program wouldn't be damaged too badly in the process.

On December 18, we scrimmaged in the Cook Pavilion, our indoor practice facility. The indoor practice field cost $3.5 million and was primarily paid for through the generosity of boosters. Dan Cook, from Dallas, Texas, and his family made the largest donation, therefore the name Cook Pavilion. An indoor facility is critical for any northern football program. It has helped us prepare more effectively for bowl games and given us more room for winter conditioning. The price tag for the Cook Pavilion was actually more than $3.5 million. The university administration told Bob Devaney and me that the faculty and students would be upset if we only built the facility to suit the football team. Although we only used donations from boosters and football revenue, we still needed to build something with other students and faculty in mind.

Finally, we were asked to build an entire student recreation complex that cost more than $16 million. We paid more than $1 million a year from our football gate receipts until the project was paid off. I was glad we could do something positive for the students and faculty, but I was worried we might bankrupt the athletic department in the process.

Many fans might think it was no problem to fund a building like this, but we showed a negative balance of almost $2.5 million at one point. Fortunately, we kept our football games sold-out and made enough from our television revenue to complete the project. To this day, many faculty members and most students don't realize that the recreation project was built almost entirely with football revenues and contributions from boosters without student fees or tax dollars. Very few athletic programs have done something like this, since most receive state tax dollars or student fees, or both. We are entirely self-supporting and even have been able to provide some revenue to the university.

On December 19, I flew to Grand Island, Nebraska, with Scott Stuart, a local advertising executive, in his single-engine plane. I went to see a recruit, who lived 35 miles northwest of Grand Island. He attended school in St. Paul, a community of about 2,000. He was typical of many homegrown recruits who have developed into outstanding players. He is an excellent athlete and student. He was a 6-foot-5 and 240-pound fullback and linebacker on his high school team. He was also a point guard on a fine high school basketball team. We're confident that he will develop into an excellent lineman once we get him on our weight program. The national recruiting services rate a recruit based upon the number of high-profile schools recruiting the athlete. Since few schools knew about him, he may have caused our ranking to drop with the recruiting services. However, we're sure he will help make our program better.

A few years ago, Bill Walsh, the former San Francisco 49ers' coach, was the commentator on an Orange Bowl telecast. During the game, Miami beat us badly so Bill commented that we had "too many eight-man players." He was referring to those players who come from small Nebraska towns that only field teams with eight-man programs. Ironically, only a short time later, Bill returned to college coaching at Stanford and recruited Scott Frost from Wood River, Nebraska. Wood River is a small town. They don't play eight-man football there, but Wood River isn't much larger than many towns that do.

Our 1994 and 1995 seniors were not highly regarded by the recruiting experts when they were recruited in 1990 and 1991. Yet, we won back-to-back national championships with them. Neither of the classes were even in the top 10 according to the experts. They were probably ranked between 20th and 30th in the nation on average. If the St. Paul recruit lived in Chicago or Los Angeles, he would have been heavily recruited and considered a top recruit by the "experts." We have many athletes on our team like him who develop into excellent players but are not highly regarded when recruited because they are relatively unknown.

I was pleased when he accepted the offer to play football for us. We returned to Lincoln around 11:00 p.m. Although recruiting is the most important thing that we do as coaches, we are always scrambling to get time to do it, particularly while preparing for a bowl game.

On December 20, I flew to see players in Missouri, Oklahoma and Kansas. When we arrived in Phoenix for the Fiesta Bowl, I visited with another outstanding recruit. I was glad the response from our recruits was positive, but I felt like I was moving in eight directions at the same time.

Not all the news was good. While recruiting was going well, Bill Byrne told me something that was disturbing. The Big Twelve presidents had an emergency conference call concerning whether or not they would allow non-qualifiers to participate in the Big Twelve Conference. We had been told the matter was tabled until spring, but the presidents now planned to make a decision immediately. Apparently, the president of the University of Texas organized the call and indicated that Texas was prepared to leave the Big Twelve Conference if non-qualifiers were allowed in the league. The vote was 11-1 to eliminate non-qualifiers with Joan Leitzel, the Chancellor at the University of Nebraska, casting the lone dissenting vote. I assume the other schools took Texas' threat seriously and decided to knuckle under. I couldn't believe they changed the rule in the middle of recruiting. Many recruiting decisions had already been made and now had to be reevaluated.

As of this writing, the Big Twelve excludes non-qualifiers and will not allow a non-qualifier to gain eligibility by attending a prep school. Also, they will not allow a student-athlete to take the SAT or ACT tests to gain eligibility after August 1 following his senior year of high school. The only avenue into the Big Twelve for the non-qualifier is via the junior colleges, and, even then, the non-qualifier must graduate from the junior college and transfer enough hours from the junior college to constitute 35 percent or more of his degree credits at the Big Twelve school. Often players do not transfer all of their credit hours from junior colleges, and they frequently are not well prepared for university classes by attending junior colleges. At this time, the Big Twelve has the most restrictive initial eligibility requirements of any Division I conference.

The *1995 Profile of SAT Program Test Takers* states that students coming from families with an average income of $70,000 or more will score an average of slightly over 1,000 on the SAT test. However, students from families with incomes of less than $20,000 have scores averaging from 769 to 813 on the SAT—less than the minimum scholarship standard of 820. I believe it's wrong to close the door on any young athlete who wants to play in the Big Twelve because he doesn't have a 2.5 grade average in 13 core courses or doesn't score satisfactorily on the SAT or ACT test.

Qualifying for an athletic scholarship is even more difficult now that we operate under Proposition 16, the new academic standard that went into effect in the 1995-96 school year. Proposition 16 raised the academic requirements for a Division I student-athlete from 11 core college prep courses with a 2.0 average to 13 core courses with a 2.5 G.P.A. The minimum test scores of 17 on the ACT and 820 on the SAT remained in force. There was an adjustment for student-athletes who had higher ACT/SAT scores, which allows a somewhat lower G.P.A. in the 13 core courses. There will be many more non-qualifiers under Proposition 16 than there had been before the standards were raised.

According to a study published by the National Center for Education and Statistics in July of 1995, Proposition 16 will reduce the number of college-bound high school seniors who meet NCAA eligibility requirements for athletics from 83.2 percent to 64.7 percent overall. The hardest hit will be African-American athletes of whom only 46.4 percent meet Proposition 16 requirements. Proposition 16 was also highly discriminatory along socioeconomic lines in that those students who were in the highest one-third socioeconomically qualify under Proposition 16 at a 73.4 percent rate, whereas those in the lowest one-third of socioeconomically classified students qualify at only a 42.3 percent rate.

In summary, Proposition 16 raised the academic requirements even higher, and in the process, eliminated those at the lower end of the socioeconomic scale at a much higher rate than those who were more privileged. For the Big Twelve to then decide that a student-athlete who did not qualify academically could not pay his own way to school and prove that he could do the work, made it even more difficult for those who were disadvantaged. Minority student-athletes comprise a high percentage of those in the socioeconomically disadvantaged group.

Studies by the NCAA projected that a large number of the male Division I football and basketball players who qualified prior to Proposition 16, would now no longer qualify. The pool of available athletes had definitely shrunk.

Some schools in the Big Twelve may believe that Nebraska was pushing admittance of non-qualifiers out of self-interest. We believe allowing students to prove they can do college work (as long as they are otherwise admissible) is fair and gives those athletes who are socioeconomically disadvantaged a chance to earn a scholarship by their second year at the university.

As the pool of academically eligible athletes grows smaller, it's likely that schools with a solid tradition will continue to get their share of great athletes. The schools with less established programs, however, will have a harder time building strong programs. I don't think the rules proposed at the athletic directors meeting will make for a strong Big Twelve Conference. When we compete against schools outside our conference, we will be at a disadvantage.

For example, let's say that in February of his senior year, a young athlete has a 16 on the ACT, one point short of the necessary 17. Let's say this same athlete has passed 11 core courses with a 2.3 average. He will need to pass two more core courses with better than a B average to qualify for a scholarship by the end of his senior year of high school. He can't wait until June to make his decision as to where he will go to school, because the signing date for football is in early February. In the event that he may not qualify, should he sign with a school that would allow him to enroll at his own expense and earn a scholarship after one year, let's say a Big Ten or Pac-Ten school, or should he sign with a Big Twelve school? If he signs with a Big Twelve school, he will either have to meet the qualifying standard or will have to go to a junior college, graduate from the junior college and enroll at the Big Twelve school. The odds are very good that the athlete will qualify. Most football coaching staffs will be recruiting five or six athletes who are in this situation. Four or five will qualify, one or two won't. Given the options now available many of these young people will opt not to take a chance with a Big Twelve school. It is not just a matter of not allowing non-qualifiers in the Big Twelve, it is a matter of losing athletes who are on the bubble and can't afford to take a chance on the Big Twelve.

NCAA projections show that many young people are being eliminated from scholarship opportunities who can do college work. They will graduate at about the same rate as those who are now qualifying. Increasing the academic standards under

Proposition 16 from 2.0 in 11 core courses to a 2.5 GPA in 13 core courses will improve graduation rates by no more than 0 to 3 percent, according to NCAA studies. Therefore, we are eliminating literally thousands of young people, particularly those who are socioeconomically disadvantaged; and for all practical purposes, we're not improving graduation rates. This simply doesn't make sense. In my opinion, this legislation is weighted toward elitism.

We are developing a serious gap in this country between those who have and those who have not. We cannot afford to widen the gap. Education is the best way, possibly the only way, for those who are socioeconomically disadvantaged to gain ground. Proposition 16 makes it harder for those who need an education the most to attend school.

During my coaching career, I have known hundreds of young men who came from socioeconomically deprived situations. Many of them would never have gotten an opportunity to get a college degree without an athletic scholarship.

Often it's about the middle of his junior year in high school before an athlete realizes he has a chance to attend college on an athletic scholarship. Under Proposition 16 it may be too late for him to improve academically so he can qualify for a scholarship. If he hasn't taken the necessary college preparatory courses or has a relatively low GPA in the freshman and sophomore years, it's almost impossible for him to get 13 core courses and a 2.5 average by the time he graduates from high school.

Proposition 16 puts a premium on good academic work habits, lots of encouragement and guidance in the early years of high school. An athlete is more apt to get that encouragement if he grows up in a privileged environment with educated parents who know what it takes to be academically successful at the college level.

Many major college football and basketball players come from blue collar environments. Therefore, they are hit particularly hard by the academic requirements outlined above. There is not the same impact on athletes who participate in tennis, golf, swimming and many other sports that have participants who are more likely to come from upper income families.

Bill Byrne also returned from the Big Twelve meetings and said the athletic directors voted 11-1 to establish a playoff game between the North and South divisions of the Big Twelve. In May of 1995, at the first meeting of all Big Twelve personnel, Big Twelve football coaches voted 12-0 against having a playoff. Most coaches thought a playoff game would only make it more difficult for both teams to be invited to a Bowl Alliance game. A late season loss in the playoff game would likely eliminate the losing team from being invited. When you lose in early December it is very difficult to be one of the top six or seven teams in the country, and that is where you need to be ranked for an Alliance bid.

An example is what happened to Alabama in 1994. Before playing Florida in the Southeastern Conference championship playoff game they were undefeated. They had a legitimate chance to be national champions. Instead, Florida beat them in the playoff game. As a result, they were invited to a relatively minor bowl and dropped out of contention for the national championship.

Obviously, most athletic directors didn't see things as the coaches did. Nebraska's athletic director, Bill Byrne, was the lone dissenting vote. The playoff was approved by an 11-1 margin. Apparently the other athletic directors couldn't resist the

$600,000-plus guarantee per school that promoters proposed to them. I'm sure they felt this was a sure thing. However, two teams in the Bowl Alliance, with no playoff, would probably have resulted in as much or more money to each school in the conference. If the Big Twelve happened to have the No. 1 and No. 2 ranked teams in the nation, they would play for the national championship. If the payout was similar to the 1996 Fiesta Bowl, each team would receive more than $10 million, a $20 million payday for the Big Twelve. With the Big Twelve playoff game in December, this scenario will never happen. During the past 10 years, the Big Twelve, with no playoff, would possibly have had two teams in the Bowl Alliances on every occasion but one. Apparently, coaches were going to have little input into Big Twelve policies.

During November, I attended a dinner for some of our major booster club contributors honoring outgoing Big Eight Commissioner, Carl James, and the new Commissioner of the Big Twelve, Steve Hatchell. We were shown a film of the Big Eight Conference history. It was nostalgic for me to watch some of the great athletes and big games in the history of the Big Eight. It was hard to believe that it was all coming to an end.

The new Big Twelve Conference headquarters will be in Dallas. Steve Hatchell, who was the commissioner of the Southwest Conference, will serve as the commissioner of the Big Twelve. Several Southwest Conference schools seem intent on preserving the rules and regulations from their old conference. Merging the two conferences hasn't been easy. I'm sure schools in both conferences are apprehensive about the future.

18

GOING
FOR TWO STRAIGHT

On December 23, our football team and staff left Lincoln on a chartered jet and arrived in Tempe, Arizona, late that morning. We held a practice that afternoon at Scottsdale Junior College. The weather was cool, and by the end of practice it was almost cold. I recall one Fiesta Bowl practice in Phoenix in the late 1980s when we ended practice with temperatures in the middle 30s. Normally, the weather is very nice there; however, winter is winter and you can hit some bad weather even if you are practicing in Phoenix, Miami or New Orleans in late December.

We had a light practice in helmets and shoulder pads, but we still had a freak collision that nearly cost us two starters. Reggie Baul, our starting split end, and Tyrone Williams, our starting corner, ran into each other and suffered leg injuries. Aaron Graham, our starting center, couldn't practice because he had a sore shoulder. As we began our final practices in Phoenix, I was alarmed by so many injuries.

We went ahead with our plans to scrimmage the next day despite several of our players nursing injuries. We held a major scrimmage and ran 120 plays with our top two units going against each other. Fortunately, nobody was hurt. I was relieved to make it through our final heavy contact in reasonably good shape. This was our second major scrimmage in preparation for the Fiesta Bowl. Although some teams don't scrimmage before a bowl game, we believe it's necessary to have some contact to prepare for the game. As coaches, we realize there is some risk of injury, but there isn't another way for us to maintain our timing, especially with our emphasis on the option.

I really liked the arrangements in Arizona. Scottsdale Junior College had several practice fields available to us. Everyone was very accommodating. We stayed at the Scottsdale Plaza Resort, which was managed by Nebraska fans, so they went all out to treat us well.

A major difference exists between Miami and Phoenix. Miami is extremely humid while Phoenix is relatively dry. The temperature might be 80 degrees in both locations, but the fatigue factor is much greater in Miami. We took the practice field in Phoenix and didn't miss a beat. Though the weather was warmer than it had been in Lincoln, the humidity was about the same.

When we played in Miami, it took almost four days before we adjusted to the climate. We always left Lincoln in shape, but the humidity factor simply destroyed us for the first few days in Miami.

After the scrimmage on December 24, we allowed our players to attend Christmas Eve services. We gave our players Christmas day off after looking at the scrimmage films early in the morning.

We had a Christmas dinner and had all of the players, coaches and families attend. Brian Nunns, a senior offensive tackle, was dressed in a Santa Claus suit and was the perfect Santa. Though Brian was in his early 20s, the younger kids were convinced he was the real Santa. Everyone had a good time and the food was excellent. The players took their customary 20 minutes to eat. It is amazing how much they can put away in such a short time.

On December 26, we became the target of a local radio station. They claimed to have had a spy at our practice. This person supposedly sneaked into practice and watched us run a flanker reverse pass. I'm sure they hoped Steve Spurrier, Florida's head coach, would hear about the report. It's true we ran the play, so they probably did have someone at practice. The station also sent a young woman to meet our players. They claimed she had spent time with our players the night before and was planning to see them again. This was all discussed on the broadcast. I'm sure they were trying to create an incident that would be newsworthy at our expense. We had our share of difficulty during the '95 season, and we didn't need more problems created by a radio station.

When I heard about the radio broadcast, I called as many players together as I could find and warned them about the young woman. Two of our players admitted to meeting her the night before and said she had called their room during the day. They promised to have nothing more to do with her.

I was surprised that any radio station would pull such a stunt. Apparently, the station had been trashing Nebraska. It seemed they had something against us. I can only speculate that it had to do with the negative publicity we received throughout the season.

About this time, the press reported that Lance Lundberg had

filed a suit against the university and me for injuries he had received prior to the Orange Bowl game two years before. The announcement came at a time when news of a lawsuit would receive considerable media attention. Lance never seemed to forgive me when I had asked him to apologize as a team captain for his role in the altercation that resulted when he had blindsided Leslie Dennis.

Later it was discovered that Lance suffered a broken facial bone that wasn't detected until several weeks after the game. This meant he had to have the bone broken again and reset. He did recover and joined the New Orleans Saints. I had heard that he would probably make their team, but instead he later chose to leave the Saints voluntarily.

He returned to school and we paid for his schooling, though he was beyond his fifth-year in school and we were not obligated to do so. We have an arrangement to help our players continue their education once they've exceeded their five-year NCAA scholarship limit. Our former players can return to school and have the athletic department pay for their education if they participate in a community outreach program. This program reaches thousands of young people throughout the state. We have eventually graduated over 86 percent of the athletes who have completed their eligibility here. The outreach program has enabled us to encourage many former players to complete their degrees.

At the Fiesta Bowl media day, we answered questions from the press for one hour. Several players and I stood on individual platforms with a microphone and had to answer question after question. Usually the same questions were repeated several times.

Most of the questions asked of Lawrence Phillips had to do with his off-the-field problems. He handled them well. The rest of our players did well with the press, also. By now we had handled about all of the tough questions anyone could ask.

I replied to comments by an NFL spokesman a few days later at the Fiesta Bowl luncheon. The day before the luncheon the front page headline of the local paper said that, according to the NFL spokesman, we had "trashed" an NFL practice field that was to be used in preparation for the Super Bowl. Ironically, the fields didn't belong to the NFL, but rather belonged to Scottsdale Junior College and were contracted for us by the Fiesta Bowl. Besides, we hadn't "trashed" the field as he claimed. The field was still in good shape.

It's hard to understand the NFL official's attitude toward us. The relationship between the NFL and college football seems one-sided. They draft underclassmen who are key players for their college teams. The NFL relies on the colleges to be their farm system at practically no cost. I thought they would have enough sense to handle their public relations with us better than they did.

At the luncheon, I also said that this incident was the last straw in terms of all the criticism we had received during the year. As a result, I told them we practiced barefoot earlier in the day, so we wouldn't tear up the field any further. Of course, this was said in jest. My only point was that the NFL complaint concerning the practice field was ridiculous.

On Sunday, December 31, we had another chapel service. Gordon Thiessen and Travis Turner, two former players, did the service. Gordon now works with the Fellowship of Christian Athletes and was responsible for editing and taking the photographs for this book. Travis has his own business in the Phoenix area. One gratifying thing about coaching for a long time is that you get a chance to see what has happened to former players. Gordon and Travis are good examples of some positive outcomes of athletic competition.

As I listened to Gordon and Travis talk, I was reminded of the many pluses of participating in athletics. Being on an athletic team exposes many young people to discipline and structure they wouldn't otherwise encounter. We live in a society that lacks discipline and stability. Being part of a team requires young people to discipline themselves to arrive on time for practice, perform certain rigorous activities and operate within a set of rules.

Richard Lapchick, from "The Center for the Study of Sport in Society," points out in a recent article that the peak time for school-aged children to get in trouble is from 3:00 to 6:00 p.m. Roughly 20 percent of time spent by all students involves sports activities from 3:00 to 6:00 p.m. Athletics can be a powerful deterrent to antisocial behavior.

Those participating in athletics are tested to the very limits of their physical, mental and emotional capabilities. I've learned that whenever you stretch your abilities and talents against competition, you learn more about yourself. The process of training and testing will do much to build one's confidence and inner strength. Self-esteem is often developed from accomplishment and hard work, not from vegetating in front of a television set.

Athletics often helps a young person to subordinate personal goals in order for the team to accomplish its goals. We live in a "me first" society. While society may selfishly focus on the individual, sports can teach the importance of teamwork. The biggest problem for most coaches today is convincing young people to take a secondary role on the team. Many players want to be in key positions and aren't willing to share the spotlight.

The team provides a sense of belonging and mutual caring that can be experienced in few other settings. I'm sure the reason gang activity is on the rise is the need many young people have for a sense of family or community. Everyone wants to belong to something and when the family unit breaks down young people are easy targets for gang recruitment. I'm sure athletic teams provide an important sense of unity and belonging for many young people because their families don't provide it.

As an athlete, you soon learn that adversity will happen. It's not so much a question of "Will I be faced with setbacks?" as "When will I be forced to deal with problems?" You don't win every game, you don't go through a career without injury, and there is bound to be disappointment from time to time. Dealing with adversity in a positive, pro-active manner is critical. The ability to do so is the difference between success and failure in so many instances.

I've noticed that the athletes in our program who are most successful aren't necessarily the most talented. I think an athlete with a tenacious attitude will have the best chance to succeed. Of course, an athlete must have some talent. But it's usually the athlete who never quits or complains who eventually does well. He will persevere through demotions and injuries to meet his goals.

Not only are there individual benefits to athletics, it seems to me that college athletics, in general, provides a much more wholesome and healthy environment than they did 20 years ago. Many fans would be surprised by my view. The average fan reads and sees so much negative reporting about athletes and coaches, they probably think things have gotten worse. However, I don't think this is true. Here are some observations concerning Division I college athletics that I believe to be true.

(1) Compared to 15 to 20 years ago, there is very little cheating today. We have seen almost no athletes in recent years whom we believe have been "bought." Barring alumni and boosters from the recruiting process and the addition of the sudden death penalty by the NCAA have made a tremendous difference.

(2) Graduation rates and normal academic progress have improved dramatically. Graduation rates throughout the NCAA reflect the fact that student-athletes are graduating at a higher rate than all other students. At Nebraska, in recent years, student-athletes have graduated at a rate 5 percent higher than the student body. For the past two years, the graduation rate of our football team has been nearly 25 percent higher than the student body graduation rate.

(3) Drug testing has greatly curtailed the use of recreational and performance-enhancing drugs in Division I athletics. It has been seven years since we have seen a positive steroid test at the University of Nebraska. We have never had a player test positive for a performance-enhancing drug on either an NCAA or Big Eight drug test and both groups have tested us unannounced for the past six years. We also see very few positive tests for street drugs.

(4) Medical care and safety have improved. The death rates and catastrophic injury rates in the sport of football have gone down dramatically since careful record-keeping began.

Most "problems" that we read about in athletics today are

simply extensions of the deterioration of our families and our culture. They also reflect how the media scrutinizes the behavior of athletes more closely and is often more critical than in the past.

We practiced in the afternoon on Sunday, December 31. It was one of only two afternoon practices that we had during the nine days of preparation in Phoenix. It was a practice in sweat clothes and was uneventful except Leslie Dennis tripped and fell on his shoulder and separated it. His injury was a freak accident and something you worry about happening when you take the pads off.

The Fiesta Bowl Ball was held on New Year's Eve. There was a huge crowd at the ball. The program was brief and the ball was uneventful except for a conversation I had with Len DeLuca and Dave Kenin, from CBS Sports. I was told the day before the ball that I needed to redo an interview with CBS Sports which had aired on December 16. It was supposed to air again on the pregame broadcast on January 2. This was my rebuttal to the programs aired by CBS News and "48 Hours." I didn't understand why the interview had to be redone. Dave and Len explained that some in the news media had criticized them for "compromising the standards of journalism." Since I was promised unedited time to reply to our critics, apparently this constituted a "compromise." I couldn't see how this compromised anyone, but I admit to not understanding journalistic ethics.

The people who talked to me the day before from CBS hoped I would simply drop the whole thing and not redo the interview. I liked and respected Len and Dave and told them I would redo the interview if necessary, but that I wanted to have an opportunity to respond to the criticism. I could tell that Dave and Len could sense the irony in CBS Sports being challenged on ethical grounds by people from the news side of the media.

I did my last press conference of the week on Monday morning. Over 2,000 press credentials had been issued to reporters covering the game. Every one of those reporters was required to write or broadcast something people would find newsworthy. One reporter told my friend Gordon Thiessen, who also had a press credential, how upset he was that I had closed practice. Gordon asked what he could write if he went to practice that he couldn't write otherwise. The writer told Gordon that if he were at practice, he could "make something up" if necessary. Fortunately, most reporters don't take that approach.

However, there are a few who are more concerned with a "good" story than they are with ethical conduct. Several years ago at the Cotton Bowl, I had a television commentator describe a trick formation to our opponents that he had seen at our practice. Eventually, we lost a close game to the University of Houston. I've been leery of open bowl practices ever since.

At the Monday press conference, the questions were familiar, and the answers I gave were the same that I had given all week. I think everyone was tired of the process. After the press conference, I was interviewed by Pat O'Brien from CBS Sports, and we redid my interview for the game. I thought the interview went reasonably well and I hoped CBS Sports would replay all of it on the pregame show.

After doing the interview, I visited with Terry Donahue, who had just retired as head coach at UCLA to become a sports commentator with CBS. He seemed eager to begin his new job, but was a bit lost because it was so new to him. I told him that I was sorry I couldn't give him any great insights regarding the game. I was in my usual state of mind a day or so before the game. I did not feel I knew any more about the outcome of the game than the average fan did.

As a coaching staff, we thought we were good enough on defense that Florida couldn't build a big lead early in the game. If we could stay close, we were certain that our physical style of play would wear them down and give us the advantage in the fourth quarter. Of course, we needed to keep from turning over the ball and have a sound kicking game as well.

I asked all of our senior players to meet briefly the afternoon before the game. I always meet with each senior class and let them know that I have appreciated all of their hard work and commitment. Hopefully, our players know they can count on me if they need help later in life.

Besides the usual things I share with the seniors, I let this group know how much I appreciated their efforts to pull together and keep circumstances from pulling us apart. I could tell that a stronger bond had developed with these players than with most seniors, and it wasn't long before there were a few hugs and even a few tears.

I knew when they left that room that those seniors would give every ounce of energy they had against Florida. Although I could not predict the final score, I knew the players were ready to play. The chemistry was right.

Later that day, January 1, we had team meetings, watched bits and pieces of various bowl games. We had a staff meeting to discuss our recruiting plans once the game was over.

The fan build-up was becoming noticeable around our hotel.

Lots of Nebraskans were hanging out there and were asking for autographs. Some fans even went to the players' rooms and knocked on their doors. It became a real problem as the players needed some space and didn't need to be badgered.

That evening we had a 30-minute walk-through practice at the Fiesta Bowl. I was concerned about the grass field because it was in bad shape when I checked it two weeks before. The grounds crew had made progress, so it looked like it was going to be fine.

Lee Corso, the ESPN analyst and former football coach at Indiana, speculated that Florida had an edge on us because they played most of their games on grass. Since we hadn't played on grass in 1995, Lee thought Florida would beat us. Lee's theory had some validity. However, my main concern was not the grass, it was Florida's great athletes. I didn't discuss the supposed grass disadvantage with our team. We wanted them to think that playing on grass would make little or no difference in the outcome of the game.

After a brief practice, we took our players to a movie. Usually, we let them pick between several movies that aren't too trashy. They normally choose a movie with lots of action, but they're usually disappointed by the end of the picture. There are few good movies for a football team to select. I didn't stay for this one. Steve Pederson and I checked them in and returned to the Scottsdale Inn to watch the Orange Bowl game. Florida State managed to come from behind to beat Notre Dame in the fourth quarter. I was relieved that we weren't playing in the Orange Bowl again. We really needed a change of scenery after playing in Miami four straight years.

I wandered down to the game room about 9:30 p.m. and waited for the players to return from the movie. As was usual the night before a game, we planned to have the players grab a snack and return to their rooms for the evening. They arrived in good spirits, seemed loose and confident—as usual, ate quickly and went to bed.

I slept well the night before the game. For some reason I always do. The next morning we had a coaches' meeting where we reviewed our general strategy for the game. We had gone over things enough by now that there wasn't anything new to talk about. It was more habit and ritual and helped pass the time.

Our chapel service was led by Keith Brown, a former player from Penn State, whom we had gotten to know in previous trips to the Fiesta Bowl. Keith did a nice job as he talked about Christian maturity. We had many players and some family members present.

After the chapel service, I had an hour or so before our pregame meal so I went for a walk with my 3-year-old grandson, Will. We walked and examined every cactus plant that we came to. It wasn't long before I realized that Will wasn't at all concerned about what was going to happen in just a few hours. Cactus plants were much more interesting. Will's point of view was refreshing and gave his grandfather a much better perspective on things.

I select a theme for each game, and the theme that we had chosen for the Fiesta Bowl was "attitude." I usually choose some quotes from various sources that relate to the particular theme of the week. While talking about attitude, I used a quote from Dan Fouts, a former NFL quarterback, who said, "It is hard to separate the mental and the physical, so much of what you do physically happens because you thought about it and mentally prepared for it." So much of what goes into a football game has to do with mental preparation. Top performance has more to do with mental readiness than physical preparation.

I also used a quote from Charles Simmons, an American manufacturer, who said, "Our attitudes control our lives. Attitudes are a secret power working 24 hours a day for good or bad. It is a fair amount of importance that we know how to harness and control this great force." I agree with him. When someone is totally focused on reaching a goal they're very difficult to beat. Their thoughts, their emotions, their hopes are totally absorbed in the task at hand. I had the feeling that our players had that kind of focus.

I also quoted Philippians 4:8, "Finally brothers whatever is true, whatever is noble, whatever is right, whatever is pure, whatever is lovely, whatever is admirable, if anything is excellent or praiseworthy, think about such things." It seems that so many people, particularly young people, spend time watching movies, television and listening to music that doesn't reflect that which is true, noble, right, pure, lovely or admirable. I was trying to help the players realize that what they put into their minds has much to do with attitudes that will affect behavior. Also, what they talk about among themselves, how they interact with each other, has a great deal to do with what the team attitude is. We try to encourage positive statements, comments that build up rather than tear down. It is a never-ending struggle to do this in one's personal thoughts and speech and also among members of a football team as well. We were fortunate to have so many players and coaches who were positive and constructive in the midst of the negativism that had surrounded us for much of the season.

As I talked to the players just prior to getting on the buses to leave for the game, I quoted from 2 Timothy 1:7. "For God did not give us a spirit of timidity but a spirit of power, of love, and self discipline." Gordon Fosness, a longtime basketball coach and current Fellowship of Christian Athletes State Director in South Dakota, had written and reminded me of this verse of scripture before we had left for Phoenix. I mentioned to our players that we had been given this spirit of power, had prepared well and were physically and mentally prepared to play the game. We had also been given a spirit of love that allowed us to show the concern and caring toward one another that would overcome hatred and fear. We also were a disciplined football team that practiced the right way, practiced hard, and had shown a willingness to pay a greater price than our opponents in the previous games. I thought that 2 Timothy 1:7 spoke directly to this particular team at this particular time.

On the bus ride over to the Fiesta Bowl, I felt oddly relaxed for a game of that magnitude. As we warmed up for the game, I felt a sense of calmness and mental clarity. I had no idea how the game would go, but I knew the players were confident and eager to play the game.

It was a long walk from the Fiesta Bowl locker rooms to the field, probably about 200 yards. Therefore, we left the locker room early. Although there was the usual anxiety as we stood and waited to go onto the field, it was no more than what we felt against Big Eight opponents throughout the year.

When we ran onto the field, I was amazed to look around the stadium and see it filled with Nebraska fans. Of course, it's not hard to spot them in their red clothing. Later, it was estimated that about half of the 74,000 people were Nebraska fans. While I'm sure most of them were from Nebraska, many were residents of Arizona and California who once lived in Nebraska. How so many of our fans got that many tickets, I'll never know. Our allotment was only 12,500, so about two-thirds of those dressed in red had either ordered tickets early through the Fiesta Bowl office or paid scalper's prices for tickets that could cost as much as $1,000 for a prime seat. Some Nebraska fans had bought Fiesta Bowl tickets and made airline and hotel reservations before the season began. I never cease to be amazed at the optimism and blind faith of fans like these.

We finally had the home-field advantage, after all the years of playing teams like Miami on their home field or Florida State only a few hundred miles from home. We had an unusually large number of bowl games where we were the "visiting" team. We played Arizona State in the 1975 Fiesta Bowl, LSU in the Sugar Bowl in 1985 and 1987, Miami in the Orange Bowl in 1984, 1989 and 1992, Florida State in the 1994 Orange Bowl and Georgia Tech in the 1991 Citrus Bowl. In the Citrus Bowl, Georgia Tech was undefeated and going for a national championship and the stands were filled with Georgia Tech fans.

In the Big Eight Conference, we hold the coin toss outside the visitor's locker room 20 minutes before the game. Usually an assistant coach makes the call on the coin flip. What the fans see on the field before the game is a mock toss. I asked the Florida coaches and game officials if they wanted to do the same for our game. The Florida coaches declined. Instead, they asked to have the coin toss on the field a few moments before kickoff. This always makes it confusing because both teams are so excited about the game that it's hard to locate the appropriate kickoff team members with just a few seconds notice.

We won the toss and deferred our choice to the second half. Florida then chose to receive the ball. Florida ran the opening kickoff back to their own 40-yard line. From there, they easily moved downfield with their short passing game. I was a bit nervous, as I watched them do the same thing against us that they did to nearly every other team during the season. They used an "empty" backfield most of the time. This meant they had five receivers split out and nobody in the backfield but the quarterback. Finally, our defense held them at our 5-yard line, so they were forced to settle for a field goal.

On the following kickoff, Clinton Childs fumbled the ball, then picked it up and had a good return out to our 33-yard line. We also benefited from a 15-yard penalty so we started our first possession near mid-field. We script the first 10 to 12 offensive plays of every game. This allows us to evaluate the opponent's defensive strategy against several offensive formations. By examining their defensive reaction to each play, we can decide how to adjust our offense. As each play unfolds, I talk over the defensive reaction with Milt Tenopir and Frank Solich in the press box. We moved down the field mostly running the ball and then threw a screen pass to Lawrence Phillips for the last 16 yards. Though we made things look easy, we missed the extra point. It wasn't like Kris Brown to miss an extra point, so I tried to give him some confidence on the sideline by assuring him everything would be fine. I felt he might be nervous because he was a freshman playing in the biggest game of his career. He responded with a fine kick off. Florida began another drive that ended with a touchdown, so it looked like anybody's game as they went ahead 10-6.

From that point on it was all Nebraska. Phillips showed his old acceleration and scored on a 42-yard run. Our defense responded with a great effort on Florida's next possession. We used a blitz that was particularly effective against the open backfield. Danny Wuerffel, the Florida quarterback, was sacked by Terrell Farley for a 3-yard loss and an apparent safety. But the officials didn't give us the safety, and the ball was spotted inside the Florida 1-yard line. On the next play, Jamel Williams blitzed and sacked Wuerffel in the end zone. This time there was no doubt on the safety. Now we had the lead 15-10. Frazier set up another score with a 32-yard run. There was no stopping us from that point. We scored 29 unanswered points.

Michael Booker scored on a 42-yard interception return. Kris Brown kicked a field goal with eight seconds left in the half as we put together a fine 59-yard drive using a hurry-up, no-huddle offense. We entered the locker room ahead 35-10. We realized that Florida was an explosive football team and that they could come back and win. However, the way our defense was beginning to stiffen, I thought it would be very unlikely for them to get back in the game.

The halftime was routine with everyone making the usual adjustments. I usually visit with the offense and then let the position coaches talk to their players. Defensively, each coach has time to visit with his players. I got them all together two minutes before we went back on the field. There was not much elation, but more of a quiet confidence. I encouraged our players to keep playing physical football because I knew our strength and aggressiveness would continue to wear them down in the second half. I was surprised to be ahead at the half, particularly by a 25-point margin. I assumed our style of play would allow us to take charge of the game in the fourth quarter, but not much earlier. Mercifully, the halftime was only 20 minutes long as compared to the Orange Bowl extravaganzas that often went as long as 30 minutes. Those longer halftimes sometimes made it difficult to maintain a normal routine.

Following halftime, the first series is always critical. Teams have a chance to recover physically and adjust their strategy. It's almost like starting the game over. I was hoping we would reestablish momentum early since we were going to receive the second-half kickoff. Our locker room was next to the Florida dressing room, so we had to wait as they filed out ahead of us. As I watched their players pass by me, I thought their body language showed some discouragement and some doubt. I thought we were in good shape.

We put a nice drive together to start the second half that ended when Tommie Frazier threw an interception in the Florida end zone from only 15 yards out. Not exactly what I had in mind to establish the momentum in the second half. Tommie rarely forced the ball into pass coverage, but this time he wasn't very careful. Florida went three plays and out, and we put together another good drive but failed on a fourth-and-five play at the Florida 30. I was beginning to worry that we might be letting Florida back in the game.

However, I didn't need to worry. Eric Stokes intercepted a Florida pass, and we quickly put together a six-play, 70-yard drive culminated by Tommie's 35-yard run up the middle on a quarterback trap. We were lucky. Florida blitzed and Tommie was home free after he cleared the line of scrimmage. When you blitz, your secondary has to cover receivers man-to-man, so Florida's defensive backs were out covering our receivers when Tommie ran through the middle untouched for a score.

Two and a half minutes later, Tommie made one of the most remarkable runs I have ever seen. He carried the ball on an option around the right side, broke two tackles, and looked like he was stopped for about a 10-yard gain as four different tacklers held him. Somehow he broke free and went 75 yards for a touchdown. His run broke the game wide open. I knew we would win the game at this point. The only question was, "by how much?"

We played many players in the second half. Brook Berringer came in at quarterback about the middle of the fourth quarter. I was really pleased we got to play him. Brook scored on a quarterback sneak. I seldom pay attention to who might carry the ball when I call a play. In this case I did, as I wanted Brook to score in his last game. Before the game, I really agonized about how to use Brook in the bowl game. Brook had been a significant part of our team's success. He deserved to play, yet quarterback is a position where you can't break continuity simply to get a player in the game. We even finished with our third quarterback, Matt Turman, playing a few plays toward the end of the game. Matt kneeled down at the Florida 1-yard line with about 30 seconds remaining in the game and that was the final play. We could have easily scored, but felt at that point we had all the points we needed and didn't need to rub it in. We played all the I-backs that we had suited up. Clinton Childs, Ahman Green, Damon Benning and James Sims all made contributions as the game unfolded and our fullbacks all had a chance to play as well.

Offensively, we ran for 524 yards and a remarkable 7.7 yards per carry average. I was disappointed that we had two passes intercepted and missed completing two passes that could have been easy touchdowns. One of those was thrown by Lawrence Phillips on an option pass where Reggie Baul was 15 yards behind all of the defenders. Lawrence is normally a good passer, but this time he rushed the pass and badly missed the mark.

Defensively, we only gave up one big play, though it probably shouldn't have been a touchdown. The replay showed their receiver was out of bounds when he caught the pass. The defender was Michael Booker, who otherwise had a tremendous ballgame. On several of our blitzes we rushed five players, bringing one extra player off the corner and still maintained a zone coverage on some crossing routes inside. This was a relatively new wrinkle for us and at times seemed to confuse Florida, especially on their pass blocking. We sacked their quarterback seven times, which accounted for part of the reason they had negative rushing yards. It's nearly impossible to win a game with so many sacks and negative rushing yards. We also intercepted three passes and recovered a fumble on a muffed punt. By the end of the game we had beaten Florida soundly in every phase of the game. I would not have thought it possible to win by a 38-point margin before the game began. The 62-24 final score was truly surprising.

It was just a few years ago that a sportswriter said we ran the ball too much, after we were badly beaten by Miami. He referred to our "scorched earth policy." Many fans and writers speculated that we would never win a big game unless we passed more. During the past two years, we have beaten passing teams from Florida with a healthy dose of the run mixed in with play-action passes. The biggest difference in our team has been an improved defense. There are lots of ways to win football games. It all comes down to execution, players and attitude.

Tommie Frazier had a great game. He ran for 199 yards on 16 carries and was named the outstanding player of the game for the third national championship game in a row. Lawrence Phillips played very well in his first start since September 10. He was under a great deal of scrutiny and responded as I thought he would.

I recall when Lawrence played against UCLA as a true freshman and carried the ball 28 times in a 14-13 win. I thought about how he played against Kansas State when Tommie was out and Brook was injured. Everyone in the stadium knew that Lawrence was going to carry the ball most of the time, and he did it with a thumb that was so badly injured that he couldn't even grip the football with his right hand. One thing about Lawrence, he would compete.

At the postgame press conference, I mentioned how proud I was of our team and said some complimentary things about Florida. I also said, "I'd like to say this respectfully to the Big Twelve Conference presidents, I hope they'll take a look at the fact that we (the Big Eight) have four teams in the top ten. We did it with Big Eight rules. We hope very much that they will reconsider and try to let the Big Twelve play with Big Eight rules and not change things because we think it makes for a strong conference."

Some writers took offense that I would use the attention surrounding the game to voice my concerns about the Big Twelve Conference. One said my comments were "arcane." I probably should have kept my mouth shut, taken the trophy and gone home. I'm sorry some people thought my comments were self-serving, but my main concern was for a strong league.

When we returned to the hotel, I went right to my room and

avoided the crowd gathered in the lobby. I'm never in the mood to be around many people after a game. My family members joined me and had something to eat as we had a nice time discussing the game.

Nancy, my son Mike, my daughter Ann, my daughter Suzi, and their spouses along with my two grandchildren had been in Phoenix all week. It was great to share this time with them.

If I have any regret about having chosen a career in coaching, it would have to be the amount of time it has taken me away from my family. Someone once said that few people will regret not spending enough time on their careers when they're on their deathbeds. However, many will regret not spending enough time with their families. It's odd how often we fail to see what is really important to us until it's almost too late.

I tried hard in the off-season to make up to them what my absence during the season took away. But even then, I probably spent too much time fishing.

Nancy has been an exceptional wife and mother as she has handled football and me in a way that very few could. I'm proud of the way our children have turned out. They have endured criticism and, at times, unrealistic expectations because I'm their father. I have been greatly blessed in this area of my life.

We finally got our bags packed about 2:30 a.m. to prepare us for our 9:00 a.m. departure. My final press conference was at 8:00 a.m. I lay on my bed the rest of the night with my eyes open. Even if others don't think I get too excited about a football game, I really do. It takes me several hours to unwind following a game. Night games are the worst because I seldom sleep until dawn.

Fewer reporters attended the final press conference, and none of the questions were too tough. I sensed some in the national press had changed their opinion of our program.

When we returned to Lincoln, we went to the Devaney Center where 8,000 fans greeted us. Since it was a work day and school day, this was an exceptional turnout considering we had won the national championship the year before and the novelty of a national championship had worn off.

Several players talked at the reception for our team. The two Sears trophies were present and Steve Pederson made sure the assistant coaches were on stage with the players and me. The year before at the national championship celebration in the Devaney Center, I felt badly because the assistants were standing in the crowd while so many others were on stage. I have an outstanding staff that has stayed together. We do most everything by consensus and I value their input greatly.

George Darlington, our secondary coach, has been with me since I became head coach 23 years ago. Milt Tenopir, our offensive line coach, has served here 22 years. Charlie McBride, our defensive coordinator, has been here 19 years. Frank Solich, assistant head coach, has completed 17 years and is a former Nebraska running back. Dan Young has coached our kickers and offensive line for 13 years. Tony Samuel played defensive end for us in the 1970s and has coached here for the past 10 seasons. Ron Brown has coached receivers for nine years. Turner Gill, a former quarterback in the early 1980s, has been back at Nebraska coaching quarterbacks for the past four years. Craig Bohl, another former player, has been coaching linebackers for one year. Steve Pederson, Associate Athletic Director in charge of football operations, has been here two years, is a Nebraska graduate and worked for us previously in the 1980s.

This staff has stayed at Nebraska primarily out of loyalty. Nearly every one has had opportunities to leave at a higher salary. Loyalty is in short supply in many organizations these days, and I greatly appreciate their allegiance to this program.

In nearly every case, I hired them because I knew them as former players, former graduate assistant coaches or as high school coaches that I had observed over a period of time. Universities rely heavily on search committees to fill vacancies. Often it is very difficult to know a person's true character unless you have worked with him or her over a period of time. I've been fortunate that I have not been bound by a search process in hiring the staff that I now work with. I hope that the university will reward them for their loyalty in the future. Most of them have given the best years of their careers to this program and have been responsible for its accomplishments.

The two consecutive championships were due to a group of players who were on a mission, a coaching staff that was unusually focused and competent, a great supporting cast of strength coaches, academic counselors, medical team, administrators and fans.

The night before the celebration at the Devaney Center, at the postgame trophy presentation, a CBS reporter asked me about winning the national championship after all the controversy we had been through. It struck me as odd that only minutes after we had won our second consecutive national championship, and had won by a surprising margin, that the subject of controversy would be revisited almost immediately. I responded, on behalf of all of our coaches and players, I think, when I told her, "We'll take it."

EPILOGUE

On Thursday, April 18, 1996, my secretary, Mary Lyn, tracked me down as I was coming in from a workout. I knew something was wrong when I saw the pale and worried look on her face. She told me Brook Berringer's plane may have crashed not far from Lincoln near the rural town of Raymond, Nebraska. Immediately, I told several assistant coaches. All of us had a sinking feeling because the facts appeared to indicate that Brook was on the plane.

The two people involved in the plane crash were not identifiable because the plane burned once it hit the ground. Turner Gill got Brook's dental records and the mold of his mouthpiece, and Turner, Ron Brown, Frank Solich, and Art Lindsay, an acquaintance of Brook's, jumped in my van, and we drove north of town to find the crash site.

When we arrived near the crash site, we saw the police cars and were escorted down a narrow private road. They took us to a field where the metal frame of the plane was about all that was left. After we gave the sheriff Brook's dental records, we stayed at the crash site for a brief time.

Once we returned to Lincoln, I made a very difficult phone call. I called Jan Berringer, Brook's mother, in Goodland, Kansas. Brook's father, Warren, had died when Brook was seven, and his funeral had been exactly 15 years before the day of the plane crash. I told Jan there was no positive identification; however, most indications were that Brook was involved in the plane crash. I could hear the fear in her voice. When we finished talking on the phone, I knew she was convinced, as I was, that Brook was gone. Later, it was confirmed that the other crash victim was Tobey Lake, a friend of Brook's and the brother of Brook's girlfriend, Tiffani.

A Fellowship of Christian Athletes banquet was scheduled that evening. It was to be a spinoff of the celebration of the national championships. Therefore, we had several players speaking at the banquet, Brook included. I went to the banquet with a very heavy heart hoping against hope that Brook would somehow show up at the banquet. When he didn't appear, I knew for sure that he had died in the crash. Brook was the type of person who wouldn't have been late for a commitment unless something catastrophic happened.

Players Mike Minter, Tony Veland, Aaron Graham and Aaron Penland were on the program that night along with our receivers coach Ron Brown and me. We were all hurting badly. I got the four players together and we had a brief prayer in hopes that we would have the strength and the poise to get through the evening.

Before the banquet, the FCA staff decided to give each speak-

er a copy of the painting called "Influence." This picture has sym-
bolized the positive influence that athletes have had in our society during the past 30 years. All seven portraits were placed in
front of the speaker's podium before the banquet began. The
"Influence" picture shows a young boy wearing an oversized football jersey. The boy is holding a football and looking toward a
small group of older athletes sitting in a circle discussing the
importance of their faith and sports. The young boy's jersey is
number 18. Of course, this was the same number Brook wore for
Nebraska. While many might think this was an incredible coinci-
dence, I believe most of our players and coaches felt it was more
than coincidental. Brook was as fine an example of a positive role
model in our football program as we have had during my coaching career. Though unintentional, the "Influence" pictures were a
fitting tribute to Brook's memory.

Authorities notified me during the banquet that Brook and
Tobey had been positively identified as the two victims in the
plane crash. Immediately, I called Jan Berringer from the basketball coaches' office in the Devaney Center. I notified her that the
identification was positive—Brook had died in the plane crash
along with Tobey.

We talked for about 15 minutes. It was one of the more difficult conversations I have had. Jan is a very strong person, and at
no time did I ever see her fall to pieces. Her three children were
her source of pride and joy. I know that she put everything she
had into raising them once her husband had died.

Right after talking to Jan, I went to a press conference. Many
members from the press were waiting in the hall and I knew that
eventually I would have to talk to them. So, as the banquet went

on in the main part of the basketball arena, I sat in the press room and talked about Brook and the plane crash. I didn't know Tobey personally, so I couldn't say much about him. I managed to make it through the press conference. However, it was very difficult for me to hold back the emotions that were welling up inside me. Brook had been a very important person in my life and I was really hurting at that moment.

I couldn't help but think about his junior season when he had played with a collapsed lung and had shown such remarkable poise and courage through a difficult time. I also thought about his unselfish attitude during the 1995 football season. Although he played at times, Tommie Frazier returned to his starting position leaving Brook in a reserve role. Because Brook was very competitive, I knew he must have been disappointed by his lack of playing time. Few players could have handled it as well as Brook did. I also couldn't help but think of our many discussions of his hunting and fishing activities and his great enthusiasm for the outdoors, something that I shared as well.

The celebration for the national championships in football and volleyball was to be held in the stadium on that Friday, the day after the plane crash. We were going to have a country western band, Sawyer Brown, participate in the festivities, and Brook was to have played his guitar with them. The musicians in Sawyer Brown were friends of Brook, so he had something to do with their being part of the celebration. It was going to be a big evening for everyone. The celebration was canceled because we realized no one in the football program could really celebrate anything so soon after Brook's death.

It was decided that the money for the celebration tickets sold in advance would be donated as a memorial to Brook. Any fans who wanted their money back from the canceled celebration could have their money refunded; however, very few asked for their $3 back. Nearly $100,000 was raised in Brook's memory.

Saturday, April 20, was the day of both the spring football game and the NFL Draft. Jeff Schmahl and Dave Finn, from our video department, brought a video to our morning staff meeting. It was a four-minute portrayal of Brook. The video showed him as a hunter, a football player and someone who cared about children. Jeff asked us if we felt it was appropriate to show the video before the start of the spring game as a tribute to Brook. As I watched the video, I was deeply moved by seeing Brook involved with the things and people he loved. I had a tough time holding back the tears. During the years I had known Brook, I had grown to respect and love him a great deal.

We decided to play the video during the pregame ceremonies with Brook's former teammates on the field. We also had many players who wore T-shirts with number 18, Brook's number, under their jerseys during the game. The mood was very somber as we prepared for the game, and I am sure many players didn't feel much like playing. When the video of Brook was played before the game, there probably weren't many dry eyes in the stadium. Nearly 50,000 people attended the spring game, the most that I could ever remember being there.

Although many of our players felt sorrow at the loss of Brook, each of them played with great intensity during the game. It was only fitting for them to exemplify the same spirit with which Brook had played. At halftime, Nebraska Governor Ben Nelson read a pledge to parents to encourage their children to avoid alcohol, tobacco and drugs. Tommie Frazier read a similar pledge for young people to abstain from alcohol, tobacco and drugs.

As I watched several thousand children take the pledge, I thought about how Brook had spent much of his time speaking at school assemblies across the state to so many young people. Ironically, the NFL draft was taking place while we played the spring game. Neither Brook nor Tommie would be drafted by the NFL. This was an amazing turn of events when you consider how much these two players contributed to our back-to-back national championships. Both had exceptional skills, and both were projected to be early draft picks. A recurrence of the blood clot in Tommie's case had scared off the pro scouts. Tommie was later signed by Montreal in the Canadian Football League. Of course, Brook's death had eliminated him from what was to be one of his finest days.

The tragic thing about Brook's death was that he had everything going for him. He had graduated in December, had an exceptional family, had a wonderful girlfriend and was about to begin an NFL career. He intended to use his professional earnings to help his family. Brook wanted to reward them for all of the years they had backed and supported him. He especially wanted to help his mother. She had taught school for 29 years and, at times, had worked two other jobs at night to pay for his older sister's medical schooling and his younger sister's college education.

On April 22, approximately 50 University of Nebraska players and coaches departed on a bus to Goodland, Kansas, to attend Brook's funeral. It was a double funeral for both Brook and Tobey. Approximately 4,000 people attended the funeral in Goodland. His hometown of 4,900 people followed everything

Brook did on the football field at Nebraska. Turner Gill, Ron Brown and I spoke at the funeral, along with others who spoke for either Brook or Tobey. The service lasted nearly three hours. During the service it was easy to see why people thought so highly of Brook. A consistent theme emerged from each person who spoke about him.

Brook enthusiastically enjoyed each day of his life. He particularly loved nature, hunting and fishing and his two hunting dogs. He had a passion for flying. Brook loved his family very much and was close to them. He enjoyed athletics. And Brook loved God. Brook was a thoroughly committed Christian who was working hard to mature in his faith. Although Brook wasn't drafted by the NFL, each of us who knew him well were certain that he was in a much better league. He was with both his earthly father and his Heavenly Father.

Brook's character was outstanding. During the funeral service, I said, "I've coached more than 2,000 players, and there is no one I coached who had better character than Brook Berringer." He was a transparent individual who was honest in his relationships and was exactly the person in private that he appeared to be in public. He had great courage. Brook was friendly to everyone who met him and was particularly good with young people. He made many appearances at hospitals, school assemblies, and other places where kids appreciated seeing a well-known football player.

Brook's position coach, Turner Gill, read a letter he wrote to Brook after his death. Turner said he imagined Brook sitting next to a tree where Jesus was talking to children. "I picture you in tall grass, intrigued by all of God's creation and of you so enjoying it.

You must feel such joy now. I love you, Brook, and I miss you. Until the time we meet again, save a place for me by that tree. I will be there some day." By the hesitation in his voice, I could tell it was very difficult for Turner to finish his eulogy.

Receivers coach Ron Brown, who recruited Brook, also spoke at the funeral. Ron said the highlight of Brook's life was August 24, 1995, the day Brook committed his life to Jesus Christ. This also happened to be his dad's birthday. Coach Brown said, "We know how excited he got about flying, hunting and fishing and throwing touchdown passes. But this was the most momentous day of his life. God allowed Brook to throw one more pass today. The question is simply this: Will we receive it?"

Coach Brown and the others who spoke about Brook knew he was well prepared for death because of the way he lived his life, and most importantly because he had already received God's pass of salvation—Jesus Christ.

To many, the crash represented a tragic, random, senseless act that was utterly final. To others, Brook's life had special meaning as he was a great example of how to live. There were still others who took comfort not only in the quality of Brook's life but also in the fact that he was committed to his faith in Christ and had his spiritual priorities in order. If there was any player on our team who had to go, Brook was probably as well prepared as anyone I know. The difficult thing was that he was so young, so talented, and had so much ahead of him.

Although Brook's life was short, he had a great impact on other people much like his father had on him. Warren died of cancer when Brook was seven, yet Brook often spoke of him as though his father had been with him his whole life. Warren had taken Brook hunting when he was very young and from those experiences Brook developed a great love of the outdoors. Warren had also shown interest in athletics, and Brook carried on that interest. Warren had been a strong Christian and Brook always appreciated the values his father instilled in him.

Though his relationship with his father was brief, it had a great impact on Brook. I believe that although Brook's life was brief, the quality of his life will have a tremendous impact on all who knew him and loved him. I know that my life has been blessed by having known Brook Berringer.

On April 25, Jan Berringer and her daughter, Drue, held a press conference in Lincoln. They thanked the many fans and people from Nebraska who expressed their sympathy toward her family. As I watched Jan during the press conference, I was amazed at her composure and strength as she calmly discussed Brook and what his life had meant to her and to other people. The whole event brought tears to my eyes as I knew how much Brook meant to her and was also very aware of how much he meant to me personally. I am known for being unemotional, yet I have shed more tears over Brook's death than anything that I can remember in recent years. It has been very difficult for all of us who knew him and cared about him. Although we have grieved for Brook and his family, we have been sustained by the quality of his life, the love he shared with his family and friends, and his faith in our Lord.

St. Louis picked Lawrence Phillips as the No. 6 choice in the first round of the NFL draft. Because several teams were concerned about his reputation, he wasn't the first draft choice. Although

I'm sure Lawrence would have liked to have been picked higher, but I think there will be less media scrutiny in St. Louis than a city like New York. According to some experts, Lawrence's off-the-field problems cost him a large amount of money. Tyrone Williams was also selected on the first day of the draft. He was taken by the Green Bay Packers in the third round.

On April 21, the second day of the draft, Aaron Graham was taken in the fourth round, Christian Peter in the fifth, and Doug Colman and Tony Veland in the sixth round. Although Nebraska had many players drafted, we did not have the type of draft that reflected our back-to-back national championships. There is no question that the focus and chemistry of our football team carried us above and beyond what our talent might have been.

On April 24, the New England Patriots announced they were going to drop Christian Peter as one of their draft choices because of his previous record. Christian had been selected in the fifth round of the NFL draft on the previous Sunday. This move was unprecedented. I was dumbfounded. Professional teams are exhaustive in their examination of the backgrounds of anyone they are considering in the draft. Christian's history had been written about and discussed in so many news outlets that I found it inconceivable that they could have drafted him and not known everything about him. Christian had spent many extra hours at the NFL Combine in Indianapolis answering all questions about his past and even providing information that was not requested.

I don't have a problem with a team passing a player in the draft if they have legitimate concerns about his ability or character. I do have a problem with a team that drafts a player only to drop him a couple of days later because of outside pressures. I believe it's wrong for a team to allow special interest groups to decide the fate of their players.

Immediately I called the owner of the Patriots, Bob Kraft, who was "unavailable." I know Bill Parcells, the Patriot head coach, and was sure that he was not involved in the decision. From what I know of Bill, he would never have handled the matter in that way. Once Christian was drafted, the same old allegations, true or not, resurfaced in the media and the Patriots apparently didn't want to live with the consequences.

The next day, I reached Kraft by phone. I told him that I was sorry that I had not heard from the Patriots before they released Christian. The Patriots' post-draft decision not to honor their draft commitment to Christian eliminated any possibility of his being drafted by another team.

Christian had been labeled as unacceptable by an NFL team, so it would be more difficult for him to catch on with anyone else. Mr. Kraft said that he thought Christian would be fine and that someone would pick him up. I suggested that even if this did occur, he was damaged goods because of the way he had been treated by the Patriots. I went through the general history of Christian's behavior and told him that many charges leveled at Christian were never substantiated. I also told Kraft that Christian had done quite well for the past three years except for the recent incident in Kearney.

Mr. Kraft had very little to say except that he would possibly contact me later and that he had to be careful of what he said. I could sense from the whole conversation that the matter was final as far as he was concerned.

Early on Thursday, June 13, Lawrence Phillips was arrested in

Los Angeles for driving under the influence of alcohol. After completing a training camp with the St. Louis Rams, he had returned to Los Angeles to pack his belongings for a return trip to St. Louis. Apparently, he had been with some of his old friends and drank too much. When I heard about his arrest, I was both saddened and upset. Lawrence not only let himself down, but he had also let down those who had supported and counted on him. I have no doubt that he has learned something from his past mistakes. It appears, however, that he still has much to learn. His options are decreasing and his back is against the wall. I hope and pray that somehow he will overcome his problems.

I am sure the naysayers have had a field day with Lawrence's arrest. I am also sure the Patriots have received many accolades for the "message" they have sent by dropping Christian from their draft. Those who clamor for this message to be sent know very little about Lawrence Phillips or Christian Peter except what they have read or seen on various news reports.

Many young people currently have very different views concerning civility, profanity, violence, honesty and promiscuity than the previous generation held. Castigation will not do much to change behavior. Modeling and expecting better behavior in a supportive environment will. Changing behavior rather than condemning it is an important part of the educational process. Coaching is about teaching and educating as much as it is about winning and losing.

In 34 years of coaching, I have yet to have a parent ask me to use their son to "send a message." Rather than asking me to make an example of their son they almost without exception have asked for mercy. Sending a message is usually reserved for someone else's children. I wonder how those who have been so strident in their demands to send a message would react if their child was the vehicle by which the message was sent? Most parents know they may be only one phone call or one evening spent with the wrong group or one poor decision away from having a child in trouble. I believe that when a parent entrusts his or her child to this football program, that young person should be treated as I would want my child treated. This does not mean that my child is to be above the law but that he is loved and cared for in a responsible way, and, if the situation called for it, is given a second chance.

It is not just children or college football players that deserve a second chance. I believe we all need to be more forgiving and understanding of each other. What each of us does with a second chance is up to us.